Escape and Return

Trips to and Memories from Roth, Germany

WALTER ROTH

ISBN-10: 0615756247
ISBN-13: 978-0615756240 (Walter Roth)

DEDICATION

This book is dedicated to my wife, Chaya, and our children, their spouses and my seven grandchildren.

CONTENTS

PART II

PART III

PREFACE

It is my strong belief that my attachment to my ancestral roots has only added to my ability to understand my existence. Since 1952, I have had the great fortune of traveling many times to Israel and Europe, including my home town of Roth, Germany. On many of these trips, my wife and other family members have accompanied me. The more time I spent with them in these places, the more I talked about my childhood and thus the I remembered more about times long ago. I have compiled over the years many notes, stories, interviews and facts relating to the village of Roth and the long ancestry of my family members who lived and worked in Roth their entire lives. Additional support came from the Arbeitskreis Landsynagoge Roth e.V., an organization that actively works to preserve the history and memories of the Jews of Roth who perished tragically under the Nazi regime.

Each time I have returned to Roth, I feel very connected with its land and its history. While I've had various issues interacting with some of the older generations in Roth, it fills me with great hope to see younger generations of Germans actively participating in the activities sponsored by the Arbeitskreis. I have even seen some of my own grandchildren connecting with children of their own age in Roth through these activities. I feel strongly that relationships developed between children bode well for the future. My love for Israel and the Jewish people is in no way diminished nor is it in conflict with my optimism for these relationships. In fact, I think it is through this appreciation for both Israel and the work I've witnessed in Germany that I have drawn much strength and comfort. It is of great satisfaction to me that the Jews of Roth are, and will continue to be, acknowledged and remembered as part of the Village's history.

ACKNOWLEDGEMENTS

I want to give a special thanks to my wife, Chaya, who has written of her own experiences during the Holocaust in her book, The Fate of Holocaust Memories: Transmission and Family Dialogues. She has been a source of great assistance and support during my compilation and writing of this book. I also cherish the participation of my children, their spouses and my grandchildren. It means so much to me that they worked through the manuscript with me. I thank my brother Herbert with whom I experienced many of the travels in this book; he generously made available to me much of his own historical research relating to our ancestors. My sister, Helen, shared with me many of her own memories and artifacts which have added a great deal to this book. Additionally, Helen's husband Lowell deserves thanks for translating the letters from my family as included in the third part of this book.

I also must thank Annegret Wenz-Haubfleisch of the Arbeitskreis Landsynagoge Roth e.V. who provided comments on my work and supplied historical materials related to Roth and Hesse area. My thanks also go out to Gabi Schmidt, and other members of the Arbeitkreis. Dan Sharon, Dr. Susan Shapiro as and Merrill Freed must be thanked for their proofreading and valuable feedback. Lastly I want to extend my thanks to my editor, Matthew Miller, who assisted me in compiling and editing my writings, notes, anecdotes, artifacts and stories into this book.

PART I:

ESCAPE AND RETURN

1

INTRODUCTION AND BACKGROUND

My ancestors belong to the long and tragic history of the Jews of Germany. At the dawn of the eleventh century, Jewish communities were strung along the Rhine, as well as in the adjoining territory of France. The Jews had been in France and in Germany along the Rhine for centuries. They were among the traders of Western Europe and had prospered under Charlemagne and the Carolingian emperors. They enjoyed the protection of the Empire and, while at odds with the Church, they lived in their communities, for the most part, without physical disturbances.

All this changed when the Crusaders burst upon the Rhineland communities in the eleventh century. Two hundred years later, even greater massacres decimated the German-Jewish settlements as the bubonic plague swept over Europe. Jews were blamed for poisoning the wells, thereby causing the Black Death. Jews were given an ultimatum to convert to Christianity and those who did not comply were slain by the thousands or forced out. They were driven from scores of German cities and towns. Many Jews left their German homeland in those terrible years and accepted the invitation of the King of Poland to settle in his kingdom.

Some, however, did not flee. Small remnants of long-established communities remained in small towns and villages in various parts of Germany, such as Speyer, Worms and Mainz. From these remnants arose the Jewish communities of Frankfurt and, later, of Berlin. There is some indication that the Jews in the area of the Village of Roth (near the town of Marburg) had trekked there from the Mainz area under permission of the Bishop of Mainz, whose jurisdiction encompassed this area in Hesse, a province of Germany, during the Middle Ages. A few Jews could be found in hundreds of small villages throughout Hesse by the seventeenth century. These Jews were, of course, constant pawns between the Holy Roman Emperor, the Bishop, the local prince or ruler (Landsgrave), and the local feudal landowners. In the Roth area, the land was owned by a family named "Schenk" (or Schenken in the plural collective). Jews had to pay taxes to one or another of these "taxing bodies" from time to time, starting from an initial tax on the right simply to live at all in a given area. But somehow from the time of the Protestant revolt and the Thirty Years War, persecution diminished and relations between the village Jews and the peasants improved.

It was during this period, in the late 1600s, that the first Jews settled in Roth. Jews had been limited to the role of petty traders and were often driven from one village to another. For example, in 1744 most Jews were ordered expelled from Roth, but one family, the Seligmans, eventually returned. With the advent of the French Revolution, and with Napoleon's creation of the Kingdom of Westphalia in 1807 in the region which included Roth, Jews began to learn trades and speak German both at home and in their synagogues. They owned and cultivated fields and farms (as did my ancestors), and dealt in trading of all kinds, especially in soft goods and cattle. Jews had started to become an integrated and integral part of the German society with some political and socioeconomic mobility.

During the nineteenth century these village Jews lived in their religious, or "holy communities" (as history refers to the Jewish communities of Worms). Their lives were built around the Torah and synagogue. They had their own schools, *mikvah*, cemetery and judicial remedies. Judaism and piety was their way of life and very existence. They were rooted to the land and lived among the peasants, with whom they traded but did not otherwise mingle. It was during this period that the house in which I was born was bought by my great-great-grandfather, Herz Stern, in December, 1832.

As emancipation increased in Germany at the end of the nineteenth century, many village Jews left for the cities. This did not seem to occur in Roth where most of the old families, including mine, remained. My father, Markus Roth, was actually born in Nieder-Ohmen, a village about twenty five miles from

Roth. He married my mother Selma Stern in 1922, and then moved to her Village of Roth. Strangely enough my father came from a family named Roth and moved to the Village of Roth, but was born in a village with an entirely different name.

The village Jews loyally served in the Kaiser's army. My father and two of his brothers were in the German army throughout World War I. My father told me that while he was in the German army, he was close enough to Paris (in 1914 and in 1917) to get a view of the city. My mother's brother, Herman, a boy of seventeen, was killed in action.

After World War I, the Village of Roth resumed its dreamlike existence for a few short years. My parents, Markus and Selma, gave birth to my brother Herbert, born in 1923; sister Irene, born in 1924 and myself, born in 1929. I was the last Jew to be born in Roth. Life began to change with the rise of Nazism in the late 1920's. By 1933, the Jewish communities in the province of Hesse, including the village of Roth, were already feeling the impact of Nazi legislation. The effect of these laws varied initially from village to village. In Roth, for whatever reason, there was no physical violence and on the whole, a constrained Jewish existence continued. In 1934, my mother Selma suddenly died of influenza, and my father married her second cousin, Toni Stern. They had one child, Helen, born in Chicago in 1939. Helen would be the last Jew conceived in the Village of Roth.

By 1935, however, even the Jews of Roth began to feel the effect of Hitler's rule. No Gentile could work for a Jew. Jewish children were increasingly barred from attending German secular schools. The villagers could not and would not trade with Jews; and so it went. For our family, a decisive moment occurred when an ad appeared in a Marburg newspaper, warning people not to do business with "the Jew Roth" – that is, my father - under severe penalties. This vicious ad ruined his business. Here is the text of the ad:

"We are advised:
The Jewish trader Markus Roth from Roth has purchased rye and wheat from the current year crop, from farmers, and has not made out the official purchase certificate, although he was legally bound to do this. Accordingly, his right to issue such certificates is herewith revoked. Those who sold rye and wheat to him shall be subject to legal action.

It is indicative of Jewish behavior—the Jew believes that the simplest regulations, which every German without doubt adheres to, have no application to him. Instead, this Jew decided to sabotage these market regulations, in order to inflict damage on the German folk. It is shameful behavior that German countrymen still trade with these parasites."

One example of the change in relations between the Jewish and Christian villagers can be seen in the way the village responded to the deaths in our family. When my mother died in 1934, many local peasants attended the funeral. When my grandmother Emma died in 1937, however, not one Christian villager came to the cemetery. In fact, the Christian casket maker was unwilling to make her a casket. The crudely home-made wooden box in which she was carried en-route to the cemetery leaked. It was said to be horrifying.

By 1936, Jewish families were attempting to leave Roth. We left in the summer of 1938 shortly before the outrage of Kristallnacht in which the synagogue of Roth was devastated. The Torah scrolls were thrown in the street and burnt the next day. Left behind were a number of Jewish community members, including my grandfather, Herz, who eventually went to live with my father's sister in Frankfurt. Additionally, my stepmother's mother Berta, along with her two sons, Hugo and Louis, remained in Roth, despite their best efforts to obtain affidavits and visas to escape.

Those Jews remaining in Roth were imprisoned in their own homes, only allowed to go out for one hour per day to buy necessities in a single, specified shop. They had no interaction with the outside German community beyond the shop and the Gestapo. This isolation continued from 1939 to 1942 when they were deported to a concentration camp, Theresienstadt. As far as I know, prior to Berta, Hugo, Louis and Herz's deportation, their only communication with the outside world came in periodic letters to and from my family. All of them died in the camps.

2

REFLECTIONS ON MY FATHER, MARCUS ROTH

When my family arrived in New York in the summer of 1938, my father, Marcus, had with him my step-mother Toni (who was three months pregnant with Helen), my brother, Herbert, my sister Irene, and me. He had almost no cash since all the money he received from the sale of his house had to be spent in Germany to buy furniture, clothes and gifts (for later sale in America) which were put into a "lift" and sent overseas. He was able to hide some money in the bottom of a coffee grinder, which helped a little. My father had a younger brother, Leopold, already living in New York but he and his wife carried themselves as aloof, well-bred, city snobs who looked down on the poor peasants from Germany. After going through immigration, we spent the first night in a HIAS (Hebrew Immigrant Aid Society) settlement house, even though Leopold could easily have put us into a hotel room. My parents were very angry about this and they never forgave him for this act of indecency.

We left for Chicago the next day by train. What excitement for me, to arrive in a big city and to go up and down in an elevator in the little hotel where we stayed in Hyde Park. This area had become the gathering place for German-Jewish refugees, particularly those from the smaller towns and villages. The Jews from the big cities moved up north in Chicago. Within a week or so, the five of us moved into a two-bedroom apartment on the third floor of an old tenement building. In an adjoining building lived our cousin, Otto Stern, and his family. They had arrived two years earlier from Roth. Within six months Toni gave birth to a little girl, Helen. To make ends meet, my parents took in a boarder who used one of the two bedrooms.

My father worked for a company called Guggenheim Packing, a company owned by a German-Jewish family, located in the Stockyards. This company hired several friends of my father, including Eric Stessman, and Joseph Stern, who were German refugees and close friends. Also hired was Moritz Rosenbusch, a cousin of my step-grandmother Bertha,

I believe my father's position at Guggenheim Packing was that of a butcher or boner, standing in an assembly line, cutting the carcass into desired pieces. The job involved getting up at 5:00 A.M. and taking a streetcar for an hour-long ride to get to his work. He would work an eight-hour day, finish at 4:00 in the afternoon, and did not get home until an hour later. When my father was a young man he learned his trade as an apprentice to a butcher in

Marburg. The work at Guggenheim was extremely difficult and was conducted in a cooler. Over a period of time his hard labor had a serious effect on his health. My father developed heart and blood circulation problems, later resulting in hospitalization for a nearly fatal blood clot in his leg. I had to go to the hospital at the time to sign a form, consenting to the operation on his leg to remove the clot. The doctor warned me that he might not survive it. He did survive and went back to work.

My father was a member of the Amalgamated Meat Cutters and Butcher Workmen Union of North America. His member number was 1098875. Historical research indicates that there was constant labor and racial strife in the Stockyards during the period that my father worked there, but he never talked about any of it with the family. All we knew was that he came home from work dead tired; he would have dinner that my step mother, Toni, had prepared for him, read the *Abend Post*, a German newspaper, and then he went to bed. In general, the family spoke in English together at home, but my father and Toni spoke to each other in their more comfortable and fluent German.

My father was a very warm man, and I rarely saw him lose his temper, except with my sister, Irene, who was often stubborn. She was brain damaged at birth, and had, I gather, a very premature birth. She also suffered from a number of illnesses over the years. Suffice is to say that as early as I remember, she was a constant source of friction and difficulty for the family. She was headstrong and belligerent, always refusing to do what her parents and siblings wanted. She was very slow and could not keep up with children her age. Her biggest conflicts were with my father and they argued often over every little thing. I was not much help in those days and thought of ways to avoid her and her problems, but she was always with the family and we could do nothing to comfort her or make her lot easier. Later she worked at menial jobs which she held intermittently for short periods of time. Psychiatric care was not known to us in those years, and even if it had been, there was not enough money to pay the bills.

My father had some close friends from Germany: Joseph Wertheim and Joseph Stern from Nieder-Ohmen, my father's birthplace, and a few others whom he would see socially. However, he had no hobbies that I knew of in America, except for reading the newspaper and listening to the radio. He participated in very few activities outside of his job.

I did try to get my father involved in sports, in baseball, in the Cubs and the Bears. I think he listened to what we told him about the games, but he never made it to a game with me, nor did he ever get very involved. I asked him once to take me to the Stockyards with him so that I could better understand what he experienced there. He said, "You wouldn't want to go there," and that was that. I never did witness with my own eyes the stockyards, that endless, day after day job that stole my father away from the family.

During World War II, my father used to bring home some meat which was not kosher, so we had to prepare it in special pans in the basement. We had a small meat grinder from which he used to make some sausages. This was a great boon considering sausage was otherwise unavailable to us. Some of us ate it but Toni never permitted it in the house.

My step mother, Toni, worked very hard during this period taking care of four children, including Helen, who was born on January 3, 1939. Toni also had to cater to a boarder in order to help us pay the rent. She was always in a very somber mood because she had left her mother and two brothers in Germany. They subsequently were killed in Auschwitz. Saddest of all was her habit of standing by the window, with Helen in her arms, looking out into a large field. She once told me that she stood there looking and waiting for her mother to finally come home.

Sometime I would wonder why it was that my father did not try to find work somewhere else. After all, his friends, after some years, managed to make it out of the Stockyards to do easier work. But for some reason my father did not. He wanted very much to have one of his sons open up a store with him, but that was not to be.

At this time, I was going to school, first at Ray School. As a young boy in a new country, it was not an easy transition for me. When we arrived in America, I had no knowledge of spoken English. I have distinct memories of certain kids who were less tolerant toward us refugees than others. In particular, I recall a number of times being chased down and attacked by a group of boys from the adjoining school of St. Thomas Church. They would call me "Christ-killer" amongst other anti-Semitic names.

One time, about a year after we had arrived in Chicago, I was attacked on my way home by these boys and I decided to fight back. A Jewish boy who had been with me at the time ran away from the attackers, leaving me behind to fend for myself. A young African-American boy who lived near me in Hyde Park saw the altercation and intervened, rescuing me. I was always grateful to that boy who came to my aid. We later became very close friends and over the years I saw him frequently. The cowardly Jewish boy, on the other hand, I never spoke to again.

I managed to make it through those tough years at Ray School and then went on to Hyde Park High School until 1947. I attended the University of Illinois at Navy Pier for my undergraduate studies and after only two years received my diploma. After that, I spent a year kibbutz in Israel before completing my schooling at the University of Chicago Law School. My father probably could not understand why I attended all these schools, but he never talked to me about it. He did not come to my graduation from high school or from law school. Toni, Helen and Irene came to the graduations so I was not too upset. My father had a good reason for not attending them – he could not afford to take the time off from work. This had absolutely nothing to do with him not loving his children. He cared for us a lot, and as far as I was concerned, he was such a good and decent man. One thing we did do was talk politics. I remember quite vividly a day back in 1945, running home after school to tell my father that I had just heard President Roosevelt had died. My father was home with my brother and it was a sorrowful moment. We discussed Roosevelt's death, what it meant to us, that the war was going to be over, and what had happened to our family in Germany. We had not heard from them since 1942 and we were left utterly in the dark about their fate at the hands of the Nazi regime.

We belonged to a German-Jewish congregation called Habonim, which came into existence around the time we arrived in Chicago. While my father and my step-mother went to synagogue on the Sabbath and every Jewish holiday, they were not really part of the "in-group" of the synagogue. This was probably due to the fact that they did not know the English language well enough to fit in, and had no experience in group activities in America. Worse than that, we were poor and could not make meaningful contributions – quite a contrast to life back in Germany.

We sometimes went to services at Rodfei Zedek which was not far from where we lived. I was to become Bar Mitzvah in April 1942, and my father went to Rodfei Zedek, where I attended Sunday school. I liked it there because the teacher, Mrs. Bernstein, was a really nice lady who knew that I was a refugee and she always made sure that I received a candy bar after every class. Unfortunately, in order for me to become Bar Mitzvah at Rodfei Zedek, the Synagogue required a payment of one hundred dollars. My father felt that he could not afford this expense and Rabbi Benjamin Daskal made the decision to not allow us to hold the ceremony there. Instead, we went to Rabbi Gronert of the Hyde Park Liberal Congregation. Later on in life when I was a full-fledged member of Rodfei Zedek, I mentioned this to the Synagogue's new Rabbi, Ralph Simon. He told me that Rabbi Daskal did not have any understanding of, nor use for, refugees.

By the late fifties my father underwent a serious arterial operation on his leg in order to restore circulation. He became very depressed and so anxious that the doctors prescribed shock treatment. A few years of respite followed during which he could not work but he could spend time with his new grandchildren. By 1965 his depression and anxiety returned. He was hospitalized in a psychiatric ward and one morning was found dead. Two years later, my sister Irene, who had become completely despondent after my father's death, walked into Lake Michigan to join her mother and father.

3

RECOLLECTIONS OF MY STEPMOTHER, TONI STERN-ROTH

Toni came to Chicago at age forty with three children not her own and after six months in this country gave birth to her own daughter, Helen. I remember in those early years how she used to wait for letters from her mother and brothers, whom she had left in Roth. The letters came fairly often until December 1941, when America entered the war. She kept those letters in a shoebox and I discovered them after her passing. They were, most likely, all self-censored for fear of the Gestapo. All subjects revolved around the family and obtaining papers allowing exit from Germany, never once was there mention of happenings or incidents in the village. Their very silence on these everyday subjects in the letters was indicative of the conditions of suffering, isolation and repression under which they were being written.

As challenging as life was for Toni, she managed to

successfully make the transition from village to America. She learned English fairly quickly when we first came to Chicago, taking English lessons at the Y.M.C.A. As the war ended and it became known that no one would return, Toni never talked to us about her mother or brothers. She never considered going back to Roth for a visit. "The people there are too evil," she would always say. Toni was able to absorb the blows that life dealt her, and she remained mentally alert and sharp throughout her old age. Only after discussing my trips to Roth would she sometimes begin to reminisce about her life there. She eventually opened up to me and she would become a source of information about the family and many other things.

Throughout Toni's childhood, the Stern family had lived at a number of different residences. They first lived in the Nathan family's house (renting the top floor) and then boarding elsewhere before settling into their house. There was not a lot of private space to be had, neither for the individual nor for the family. But such was life. The Sterns had no radio, or telephone. There was only one washroom which was located outside the house, making winters particularly difficult. Heat was produced by the kitchen stove. Water was boiled in a kettle atop the stove. This water was used for drinking, cooking, and bathing. Baths were taken inside a big round tub that was kept in the kitchen. According to Toni, this was not such a burden since "people did not need to bathe as much then – people just did not get as dirty as they do today!" There was also an additional stove situated in the living room to help circulate the heat during the coldest of times.

Outside of her life at home, Toni lived the life of a typical Jewish child of Roth. She first attended grammar school when she was six. Classes were quite small, as one would expect from such a small village. The largest class had twenty children in it. The schoolhouse, containing eight grades in total, was split into two classrooms – the younger children in one room and the older in another. Teachers had to be well-equipped to manage a range of students of varying ages and each teacher taught all subjects, including arithmetic, history, and science. Students arrived at eight or nine in the morning and had lessons until lunch. Afternoon lessons usually lasted from one to three, followed by an hour recess for sports or games before the school day concluded. Students rarely used notebooks in those days to practice their writing. They instead wrote on a *tafel* (a slate) using a *griffel* (a slate pencil) and erased with water and a sponge.

The Jewish children attended the same school as the non-Jewish children. About a dozen students in all were Jewish. On certain days when religious studies were being taught, the Jewish students did not have to attend and would come to school later so as to avoid these lessons. Jewish studies were instead provided by the Jewish community. Once a week the children convened in order to study Hebrew and Jewish prayer. The teacher, Josef Sweitch, was an Orthodox Jew who had his roots in Poland. He commuted into town from Gladenbach which was a considerable distance from Roth. Every month classes were held at a different house since there was no official public space provided by the municipality for these lessons. To supplement these Hebrew lessons, the Jews attended Friday night and Saturday (Sabbath) services, and also Bar Mitzvahs and weddings.

4

1953: A VISIT TO MY MOTHER SELMA'S GRAVE

My first trip back to Roth took place in 1953, fifteen years after my departure with my father, stepmother, sister, and brother from the Village. The visit was a brief half-day stopover on my way back from a year stay on a kibbutz in Israel and took place only because I wanted to stop at my mother's grave. Because I grew up in America, my mother, her grave, the Jewish cemetery in which the grave is situated, the cemetery land and Village which it adjoins, and the Jews who were once among the inhabitants of Roth all had an increasingly mysterious and magnetic pull on my thoughts. I was still too angry at the Germans generally and was not old enough to deal with the complexities of Roth, its villagers or its Jewish cemetery. My family in America was also too numbed to permit open discussion of the tragedy that had befallen the Jews of Roth who had remained after we left. I therefore never heard much about my mother, Selma.

On February 28, 1934, the eve of the Jewish holiday of Purim, my mother, named Selma Roth, age thirty five, of the Village of Roth, Germany, died in a section of a hospital in Marburg. I was then just about five years old when my father came home and took me, my brother, and my sister into a side room. I sat on his lap and he told us our mother had died. That was it. The next morning everyone walked behind a casket up the hill to the Jewish cemetery. I stood at the door with our Gentile maid, and was kept at home. I remember that I did not cry.

To say that my mother died on that day is, of course, a fact that was told to me by others. I was not with her when she passed; I do not have much of a conscious recollection of her. Certainly, she and I had a relationship as she was my mother, but somehow her departure was of such a jarring nature that all I could not recall any substantial memories of her while I was growing up. The death of a young parent must have been so unnatural, so awful, that no one in my family spoke about it until many years after the event, and then only in general terms. It's almost as if this young woman, who left behind her parents, husband and three children was erased from the conscious recollection of her children and rarely if ever spoken of by her husband. My mother Selma lies buried in a small fenced cemetery reserved for Jews on the top of the Geyersburg, a small hill overlooking the Village of Roth, where she was born and lived. Even after death, the Nazi tragedy conspired to erase her memory, for during the Second World War, the stone marking her eternal resting place vanished and the borders marking her grave were destroyed.

When I saw the cemetery for the first time in seventeen years, it was overgrown and unkempt. It was obvious that the cemetery had not been attended to after the Jews had left. There were hardly any tombstones still standing. Large bushes and trees covered the grounds. I looked for any remnants of her grave and found none. I felt outraged, disheartened, and sad and wanted to leave the site.

While I don't actually remember my mother, one of my few childhood memories, which has since come back, occurred shortly after her death. I recall that I once sat in my bedroom looking out the window and saw a creature, which looked like an angel, fluttering outside the window. It was a biblical angel, with wings. It was real to me. I ran out to the window and watched it. Then it was gone. I have never been able to go further with this image - it was real - it was full of hope - it may have been my mother. I would also often sit with my grandfather, Herz, on the banks of the River Lahn and ask him what happened to my mother. His answer would be, "Her heart stopped beating." "Where is she?" I would ask. He would answer, "In heaven – look at the clouds and you will see her." I looked at the clouds very often during those days.

The visit in 1953 was brief but significant. I took the old train with wooden seats from Frankfurt to Niederwalgern, a neighboring village. Walking from the railroad station across the fields of flowers and grain to Roth, I entered the village, around noon time. Many people came running out to the street and recognized me, saying "Das is Markus' sohn." (This is Markus' son). Some of the women were dressed in peasant garb. They began asking questions of me, about Markus, likely because the villagers all knew that he was still alive. It was apparent that they all remembered my father, but no one asked about my grandfather Herz, nor my stepmother's family. I was uneasy, and told them that my father and stepmother were fine. There was no discussion about the Jews who had disappeared.

There were some questions and statements which I found difficult to deal with and which I could not understand. One villager told me how lucky I was to have left Germany, as a number of my Gentile friends had been killed while serving in the German Army. The implication was perhaps that I had escaped service in the war just in time and obviously overlooked what would have been my ultimate fate as a Jew. Others commented that they were angry at my cousin Otto Stern who had served in the American Army and traveled to Roth immediately after the wars end. When he entered the village and discovered that the Jewish cemetery had been destroyed, he ordered the mayor to have it cleaned within a few days or threatened to return with additional American troops to enforce this order. When Otto returned days later, the cemetery had been cleared. The villagers told me how much they resented Otto's behavior as they were "not responsible for the damage done to the cemetery" and claimed it had been perpetrated by outsiders from the Nazi party.

I had paid my respects to my mother while managing to minimize my interaction with the local residents. I was only in my twenties at this time and was not at all ready to deal with the deep-seated range of emotions that I felt toward the German people. Many years would pass before my next trip to Roth; I would return more mature and prepared to engage the townspeople.

I returned home from my year abroad 1953. Since I had already graduated University of Chicago Law School, I was able to obtain a clerkship with Judge Luther M. Swygert of the seventh circuit federal court. In 1955, I became an attorney with the law firm of D'Ancona, Pflaum, Wyatt, & Riskind and married my spouse Chaya, herself born in Germany and a Holocaust survivor with her own story to tell.

5

MEMORIES RETURNING

In my first trip to Roth, memories were few. Over the passing years, as I established my life in Chicago and began a family with Chaya, lost memories began to surface. As I shared these stories and fragments with Chaya and our three children, the transmission of stories, places and remembrances to my family allowed even more memories, although sometimes disjointed, to surface. I found many provided insight into my actions, likes and dislikes as an adult. Still, more importantly they opened the way for family discussion which would eventually play a part in preparations for framing a family trip to Roth in 1982, as discussed in the next chapter.

I begin with my father, Markus Roth. I remember my father chasing a bull that had broken loose and was spotted running down the street. He caught up to it, put his fingers through the ring in its nose and walked the bull tamely to an enclosure. I was very proud of him.

I also remember my father and others gathering around a calf I loved, spreading it on the ground, tying its legs and cutting its neck with a butcher's knife. On this occasion, I hated him.

Then there was the evening when my newly married father and stepmother returned to our house while I was playing cards and I called her a bad name. My father snatched the cards out of my hands and threw them into the fire. He also slapped me. It is the only time that he ever hit me and I have disliked playing cards ever since. As it would turn out, I did many things with my stepmother and in the end we became friends. She and I went picking wild blueberries in the woods and participated in other activities together, like baking and cooking.

Of my grandfather Herz Stern, I remember him being small in stature like me. He sold linen and the like. He had the appearance of being slightly stooped, probably from years of carrying his backpack as he walked from village to village selling his wares. He was very old-fashioned and friendly. We had a mail box in the Village. Grandfather would drop a letter into it, walk away and then return to see if the letter had really dropped in. He would repeat this several times before being satisfied that the letter had really dropped. I, too, did this for years after.

The memories of Village life are fleeting but warm – sitting on a horse-drawn wagon in front with my father, while I was singing and eating rye bread spread with plum jam and sugar. I liked working in the fields with my father, stacking hay, picking potatoes or hoeing. In the evenings, we used to go up to Geyesburg, the hill outside the village, to catch maikaefer ("mayflies") buzzing and lighting up in the evening sky. During my 1984 visit, I discovered that the maikaefer had disappeared years earlier due to the use of insecticides. It also turned out that they no longer made the pflaumenmus (plum jam) or hand-cheese that we had in the old days.

I also fondly remember the synagogue to which we belonged. I loved attending services there. I would sit on the lower level with my father or grandfather or go upstairs to the balcony to be with my mother. On Simchas Torah, we had a celebration and the women threw candy to us from the balcony. Once a week Lehrer Simon, our Hebrew school teacher, would come to read and write Hebrew with me and several other children. He was a very frail man from Marburg who would bring his own hardboiled eggs and bread to eat outside our house since our kosher kitchen was not kosher enough for him. I have no fond memories of him. I have been told that he too perished in the Holocaust.

I recall that after my mother died, I slept downstairs in a little alcove in the same room as my grandmother on my mother's side, Emma. After Emma died in 1937, she was laid on the kitchen table and washed by female relatives from the Village. I was an unseen observer and it was fascinatingly awful.

Shortly within the time after my mother died, I fell running up the school steps and split open my forehead. A little later, I ran after a wagon, fell and impaled my cheek on a protruding stick. Later, I fell again and split my tongue. On all of these occasions, my brother took me on a bike to a neighboring village to a doctor so my bloody mess could be sewn up. I still have the scar on my forehead to this day.

I also recall that once while my brother and I were watching two women making jam, a boiling pot of pflaumenmus tipped over on to my brother's feet, severely scalding him while I was watching. It bothered me a great deal to see him hurt so badly.

We also had some pets. I had a dog named Erdman (meaning "dog of the earth"). When we were about to leave the Village, we gave him away to a neighboring village but he made his way back. My father gave him away again and I never saw him after that. I never had another pet, either. We also had a horse named Schimmel (meaning "moldy") that I liked. When we left the Village, they gave him to someone else. I remember him being taken away and I cried very hard.

Anti-Semitism, which was rising in the village, soon affected me in the school. When I was about seven years old I raised my hand in school to announce that I was the first one to have the correct answer to a math question that our teacher had posed to the class as a contest. The first one to raise his hand was allowed to walk in front of the room and announce the answer. However, when I raised my hand, the teacher said I could not have the right answer because I was a Jew. This experience left a bitter taste in my mouth. I have hated math ever since.

I remember that once there was a military parade of Brown Shirts through the Village. They played "Deutschland Uber Alles" and my hand shot up, like the rest of the villagers. When I put my hand up to salute, I remember someone slapping my hand to put it back down. I was also told to stop singing Nazi songs. I was too young, I guess, to understand that the Nazis wanted to kill us. This was the last time I ever put my hand up like that to salute.

Later, before they kicked me out of school with the other Jewish kids, I was accosted by some older boys who called me a dirty Jew. They took my chalk pencils and tablet and broke them one by one. I ran home crying but told no one as to what happened. Years later I told it to my father who said it could never have happened because Jews were never attacked in our Village.

My last memories of my German childhood are from our departure. When we left the Village, we went to Stuttgart. I went with my father into an examining room where a doctor examined us. The examination was to make certain that we were healthy in order to meet the requirements for an American visa. He and I stood there naked and I was very proud of my father then. We then made our way to our ship, a German liner, which left from Bremerhaven. I still remember the huge waves crashing against the breakwater as we departed at the port. I became terribly seasick on the voyage.

The big occasion during the trip was that the Joe Louis – Max Schmeling boxing match took place. The German crew was all quite involved in having their German champion, Schmeling, beat Joe Louis, the great American boxer. Joe Louis won the fight by knocking out Schmeling in the first round. We heard that Joe Louis beat Max Schmeling when we were mid-ocean. We Jews were happy that the German was defeated. However, we were also scared about what the German crew might do to us. Fortunately, nothing happened and the rest of the voyage was uneventful.

After a week at sea, the ship finally arrived at New York harbor. I stood with my father holding his hand as we sailed past the Statue of Liberty. The sight was unforgettable. Rather than landing at Ellis Island, which was closed, we landed at Pier sixty-eight where we were met by my father's younger brother, Leopold, who had immigrated to America before us.

6

1982, THE FIRST FAMILY VISIT TO ROTH: THE SECOND GENERATION EXPERIENCES ROTH

Thirty years passed and in the summer of 1982, almost half a century after my mother's death, I took my wife and three children for a somewhat longer visit to Roth and the Jewish cemetery where my mother is buried. The 1982 trip to the Village of Roth was very different than the first visit in 1953. My wife, three children (Ari, Judy and Miriam, then ages twenty-one, nineteen and seventeen) and the passage of thirty years made a great difference in my ability to sift out some of my emotions with respect to Roth. We spent two days in and around the Village, visiting the Jewish cemetery and introducing the family to a number of the villagers who remembered me. Nearly every encounter was brief – but friendly.

My wife, also of German birth, was born of Polish parents who lived in Berlin. Her father was killed in the Sachsenhausen concentration camp in 1939 and her mother had taken Chaya and her older sister, Gitta on a five-year flight across Europe, through Belgium, southern France, the Alps, and finally Rome. Like me, Chaya had great difficulty in seeing and tolerating Germany and its inhabitants. In fact, her reactions were even more intense than mine. While superficial friendliness was easy on this trip, meaningful discussion with the villagers of Roth was difficult.

One particular interlude that I recall occurred in the home of Konrad Pfeffer, who lived across the street from our old home in Roth. He struck me as a perfect example of a German peasant. He had served in the German Army in World War II, and had been wounded on the Russian front. His family had done us no harm in Roth and he claimed that his father had been a good friend of my father "in the old days." He argued that if Hitler had only not harmed the Jews, he would have been good for Germany. We vigorously disagreed, adding that the German people should have done something to stop Hitler when he turned on the Jews. He was very angry at this statement as was another villager who was present. Konrad also complained to us that the Jews of the village never ate in the houses of the peasants. When he offered us the hospitality of a meal, we declined and said we ate only *kosher food*, which was true only in part. We did, however, accept his offer of a beer.

I took the family to the cemetery on the Geyersburg. Coming back this time with them I felt more comfortable and at ease. We sat at the edge of the woods adjoining the cemetery and talked about the history of the village and the lives of our family.

Leaving the cemetery, we returned to the hotel to discuss our reflection on the Village. We talked about how it was possible that the people in the Village, who appeared so friendly to us, seemingly did not have any feelings about what had happened to the Jews who had been killed due to the deportations from the Village. It was confusing for all of us, particularly my children, to see such a beautiful landscape, meet friendly people, and at the same time, know the connection and history of the villagers and murders of our family and friends from Roth.

We did not stay in the village long. Instead, we decided to drive to Dachau, a notorious German concentration camp for political dissidents and Jews, located outside of Munich. We wanted to get a more realistic view of the German character under Hitler. The remnants of the oppression and brutality of Nazi persecution witnessed at Dachau more than balanced the "friendly" reception we had received from the villagers of Roth.

After the Dachau visit we drove off through France to Verdun. Chaya and I wanted to show our children the great underground fortress and the great battlefield where the French fought the Germans in World War I. From there we drove to Paris and later to Nice and the foothills of the French Alps to retrace the path taken by Chaya and her family. We drove to Venice and then to Italy, across the Alps, where Chaya's family had hidden when the Nazis occupied southern France. Chaya even located an elderly lady, Andreina Blua, who had hidden her family in the Italian Alps forty years earlier. Chaya writes extensively about this in her book, *The Fate of Holocaust Memories (2008)*.

My children, my wife, and I were deeply involved with and affected by what we had encountered during our visit to Germany and Italy. With that in mind, I decided I might soon need to return to Germany at the first opportunity. This occurred shortly after, only two years later, when I would go back with my brother.

7

OBJECTIVES OF THE NEXT RETURN

After I returned to Chicago from our 1982 trip, there was a great deal of thought and discussion amongst my immediate and extended family about the experiences of my most recent trip. In talking through this with my brother, Herbert, who had also visited the Village just prior to the time that I was there, we began to discuss a possible return. This would eventually grow from an idea into a set of goals.

Since Herbert was fifteen when we left Germany, six years older than I at the date of our departure, he still had several schoolmates and friends whom he remembered and who remembered him. One in particular, George, from the neighboring village of Wolfshausen, had helped Herbert a great deal in obtaining materials on the history of the Jews of Roth. George brought Herbert research material written by a German containing a great deal of information about the lives and history of the Jews in Roth, their synagogue, their school and their cemetery. Herbert had also retrieved some material from the archives in Marburg. This material opened a perspective about my forefathers which had heretofore not been apparent in my mind. Herbert dedicated a great deal of his time and energy to collecting this material, translating it and subsequently using it to frame the history of the Jews of Roth in English.

Herbert showed me some of the archival material that contained information about the Jews of villages where our ancestors had lived. This led to us talking about replacing the tombstones of our mother and grandmother. Once we decided to do this, we felt that we should go there for the dedication of the stones when they were completed. This project became somewhat more elaborate when Herbert suggested that we also erect a memorial plaque in the Jewish cemetery in memory of the Jews of the Village, including our Toni's mother and two brothers, who had remained in the Village before being deported to Theresienstadt, and from Theresienstadt to Auschwitz where they met their tragic deaths.

There was another reason why I wanted to go back once more to Germany. I felt compelled to again check on the death of my grandfather, Herz Stern (my mother's father), who had been left in Frankfurt when we left Germany. He was about seventy years old when we left, a gentle little man, whom I remembered with a great deal of affection. He had written to us a number of times after we had left Germany about his travails and his great wish to see us again. One of the last letters that we received indicated that he had been hospitalized and was quite ill. This was in 1941, before America had entered the war. He wrote in his last letter that he had had a dream in which he had seen my little sister Helen (whom he had never had occasion to meet since she was born six months after we arrived in Chicago). He wrote that he vividly imagined her wonderfully dressed in blue velvet and beckoning to him. That was our last correspondence with him, we never heard from him or about him again. There was no trace of him when I visited Germany in 1953 or when Herbert checked again in 1982. But I wanted to go back to Frankfurt to see once again if anything had turned up. We all, of course, assumed that he had died in Frankfurt in the latter part of 1941 or in early 1942.

And so I returned to the Village of Roth in the summer of 1984 with my brother for a more extended trip to the Village, with the added purposes of learning more about the Jews who once lived in the area and the dedication of the gravestones for our mother and the memorial to the martyred Jews of Roth. We were subsequently joined by our second cousin, Otto Stern, and his son, Arnie. Additionally we were joined by Trude Wetmore, who had been born in the Village of Roth, and her husband, who were now living in the Chicago area. I kept a journal of my ten day trip to the Village, which with a little editing, has been set out on the following pages.

8

1984: MY BROTHER AND I RETURN TO ROTH WITH A NEW TASK AT HAND

Herbert and I left Chicago in a torrential downpour. No cabbie wanted to go to O'Hare because of the rain and it was only after about half an hour of waiting that we got to the airport. Herbert's flight left earlier than mine and he just barely made it. My flight left one and half hours later, and it was teeming with youngsters of high school and college age. Next to me sat young newlyweds from Hyde Park who were going on a car trip for their honeymoon. They only had a vague idea of heading southwards in Germany so I made some suggestions to them. How different they were in their demands and expectations from which we required on our trip -- reservations, plans, maps, and the like.

They wanted to know about my trip and so I told them. They mentioned they had a friend at the University of Chicago who was writing a thesis on the social structure of a concentration camp (from the Nazi side I guess). I also talked to a young graduate of the University of Illinois who was going to Paris and Israel. The flight essentially was very pleasant.

I found myself again thinking about the purpose of this trip. Would it be possible to finally come to grips with my emotions relating to the German people in order to clearly see and record what I was about to experience? There I was, fifty five years of age, confused and feeling a familiar sensation from my prior trips to Roth; time was passing by while I lacked the ability to focus the experience into a meaningful picture. I had set off with the newfound belief that to obtain the most from this trip, I would need to leave my mind's expectations on the flight and just see, record, and experience our trip. I was going back once again to the Village of Roth in that elusive attempt to see it from the beginning - which was obviously not possible due to the passage of time. But somehow and somewhere in those first years of growing up in Roth, between the passing of my mother and grandmother and then leaving abruptly, the "camera" in my mind was turned off and some part of me stopped.

Day 1, June 14: On the Ground in Germany

Herbert met me at the gate in Frankfurt and before we even left the airport; we got right down to business. Rabbi Avi Weiss of New York joined us for a brief meeting on the upper floor of the airport, where we discussed and planned our dedication ceremony at the cemetery. Rabbi Weiss was a young fellow in his thirties. He was Orthodox and had recently been assigned as a U.S. Army chaplain to a post in Germany. I had connected with him by chance through an inquiry to the American Jewish Congress. After my initial phone conversation with Rabbi Weiss, we agreed to work together on a program for the dedication, which led to our first of many meetings. After the sit-down in the airport, Herbert and I departed. Herbert had rented a stick shift car which I could not drive (I had never learned to drive manual; truth be told, Herbert could only do so with some difficulty).

We first drove to Wolfshausen. Herbert went straight to the house of his boyhood friend, George, and his wife, Anna. George was an immensely pleasant fellow who had unfortunately been suffering from cancer. He and Anna had a good sense of humor, though. I remember that once when we were eating, she was in the kitchen cleaning or cooking, and George said in German, "When a woman works, she need not eat." Due to his close relationship with Herbert and his involvement in Herbert's prior research, George was very devoted to our dedication project in Roth. He showed us an article that had just been published on June 8, 1984 in a local newspaper about the dedication ceremony for which Herbert was interviewed. My name was not mentioned, however I was not upset. After all, it was George, Herbert's friend, who arranged for the interview.

While at George's we ate a bit and had some beer to drink. George then read out loud for us in "Platt" Deutsch. "Platt"

Deutsch was a dialect spoken by the villagers. Herbert was very attached to him and so he stayed at his home. I instead stayed at the local Hotel Bellevue which worked out just fine. From George's, we drove to the hotel. After I checked into my room, we met two Jewish women from San Francisco who were also visiting with their husbands. The women were born in the nearby Village of Fronhausen and had been deported to the Riga ghetto work camp in 1941. Herbert had been in contact with them prior to our trip and we were looking forward to becoming more acquainted with them and their stories. We were also hoping to meet a descendant of the Schenken family who had arranged for these women to come to Germany. We decided to delay talking with them until the following morning. We instead returned to George's for the next day's planning. After we made our plan, I recorded George reading German poetry from a well-known book, *Mein Dorf* (meaning "My Village"). I mention this as some of the contents of the poem could be construed as anti-Semitic.

My brother seemed at ease with the non-Jewish people he knew in the Village. He felt at home in this place. Unlike Herbert, I was unable to remember a single non-Jewish friend of mine. The only people that I could vividly remember were two Jewish boys who were my age. They had both been deported and killed. Yet looking across the highway at the Village and the cemetery on top of the hill gave me that same old feeling of security that used to overwhelm me growing up. I truly felt that that was where I belonged, that was my turf, my home. George's two brothers were killed in World War II in the German army, one at the age of seventeen. Strange to think that if I had not been a Jew, I might have also been killed as a soldier fighting for Germany. In 1945, they were taking boys from the Village to the frontline. I would have been sixteen then. It is thoughts like these that made me realize that my life is really a gift on many counts.

Day 2, June 15: Dedication Preparations, Our Old House and Some Old Acquaintances

I woke up the following morning fairly well-rested. After breakfast, Herbert met me at the hotel and we spoke with the two women from San Francisco and their husbands. They told us of their travails. They were young girls of approximately fifteen and sixteen when they were deported to Riga in December 1941. Riga was a work camp that had been where Lithuanian Jews were deported. It turns out that Lehrer Simon (my old Hebrew teacher) was on the same train as they. Somehow the girls survived four years of horror. Their sister, brother and mother were less fortunate. Lehrer Simon also did not survive the camp, starving to death because he refused to eat non-Kosher food. By this time, I had heard so many horror stories and so many tragedies had been recounted, that I began to feel numb.

Herbert and I then drove with George to pick up a key to the Jewish cemetery in Roth –the place I felt most at home at in the village. The mayor of Roth was already up there with a work crew that was cleaning up the cemetery and cutting the grass in preparation for the upcoming ceremony. We stared at those mystic, old, sandstone gravestones. I remember vividly that engraved upon the gravestones were the following words: "*Friede Seiner Asche*" or "*Ruhe Seiner Asche*" ("Peace to your ashes"/ "Quiet to your ashes"). Our mother's stone was to be replaced the following Thursday. Finally, she would rest in peace. We then drove to Marburg to look into renting a video-recorder for the ceremony. We tried negotiating with one photographer in particular who charged the equivalent of $900. He would not budge on the price, but we decided to settle with him anyway. After all, we did want this for posterity.

We next headed to Gladenbach to meet with the gravestone cutter who was making the stones. Herbert paid him another $1,500 for his services. He told us about the antics of a man named Rabbi Roth, whom he had gone to see in Frankfurt for a three hour meeting to obtain approval for the erection of the memorial stones. Rabbi Roth, whom we were told had authority over the Jewish cemetery, was an old man from Hungary who apparently had taken some objection to the lettering on the memorial tablet. I had previously written to this rabbi and had commented that it was quite a coincidence that his name was the same as mine and the village in which I was born. He wrote back, in an unfriendly tone, that he had never heard of the Village of Roth. He finally gave us his approval.

The memorial stones looked fine and we left for a pleasant

drive through the back country – through the villages of Lohra, Frohnhausen and Niederwalgern. We then returned to Roth, where we met and talked to Mr. Schmitz, the young journalist from the local newspaper who had written the article about Herbert's activities in setting up a memorial for the Jews of Roth. The young newspaperman was rather sincere and perceptive and was very concerned about some of the current political developments in Germany, such as the Greens, the anti-nuclear movements and the anti-foreign workers movements.

The next stop was our old house. We parked in front and went to the old barn and the backyard, where we once had a lovely orchard containing all types of fruit trees. All the trees that had once stood there were gone, but we did find the old plow which we used years ago and the wheels of the wagon that my father used to drive. We saw the German writing that was burned into the wood on the side of our house when it was built in 1774. It was Psalm 41, Verse 7:

> "Sie Konnen nach mir zum schauen, und meinen's doch nich von Herzen; sondern sie suchen etwas, das sie lasterm konnen, gehen hin und tragen's hinaus auf die Gasse"
>
> (German)

> "And if one comes to see me, he speaketh falsehood. His heart gathereth in iniquity to itself. When he goeth outside, he speaketh of it."
>
> (English)

The same verse had been repainted on the front of the house when it was remodeled by the inhabitants who moved in after we left in 1938. The current residents were the descendants of the same family that had bought the house from Dad at a coerced price when we left.

After stopping by the house, we encountered a number of locals. We met a lady whose family used to live next to the synagogue and whose mother turned lights off for the Jews on the Sabbath. Herbert bumped into Jacob Ruth on the street. He had been a good school friend of Herbert's. When he saw me, he referred to me as "Das ist der kleine" ("That is the little one"). Imagine that. That is how he had remembered me from forty five years earlier.

We then went to see Else Pfeffer who had grown quite old (she was about seventy one). She talked about how she used to take care of me when I was young. She still dressed in the typical fashion of the old-style women peasants of the Village – a white apron, a black dress and a bun hairdo. She told me that after my mother died she would often take me to her house where her mother comforted me. She also asked about my sister, Irene, and wondered what had happened to her. I informed her that Irene had since passed away.

We then went over to see Konrad Pfeffer, our neighbor growing up in Roth, and his family. I met with them during my visit two years earlier and made it a point to reconnect with them once again. We proceeded to have a long rambling discussion about politics. Konrad blamed all of the world's ills on the Americans not doing the right thing. His opinions apparently had not changed much. At one point in our conversation, Konrad said that our family's horse, *Shimmel*, was not given away as I thought. According to him, the horse had gone berserk and was subsequently slaughtered. How about that for a child's memory? I distinctly remembered *Shimmel* being led away.

Once again, we went to George's at the end of the day in order to plan the following day. I then retired to my room at the hotel where I collected my thoughts and reflected on the day's activities. I was a bit dissatisfied with the day as I had hoped to accomplish more than we had. I also realized, again, that I had no roots, history, or commonalities there with those people. All I felt connected to were some parts of the land, the cemetery and the sound of the language. Nothing else. At the time, I felt all else was dead forever.

Day 3, June 16: Old Pictures, Old Prayer Books, and more Archival Material for Herbert

After breakfast, I once again had a pleasant conversation with one of the women from San Francisco. She had such fond memories after all those years. She told me of her love for the old Baroness Schenck who then lived in Fronhausen. I can still picture her now with her eyes looking over her shoulder to see if anyone could hear our conversation. She leaned over and whispered into my ear the proper etiquette when in the presence of a Baroness: "You never ask a Baroness anything directly. Rather, you ask, 'Would you consider…' or 'are you able to…'" This of course was her response to me when I inquired whether or not we would get a chance to see the Baroness and her daughter. The women from San Francisco had a special relationship with the Schenken family, or so they claimed. The Baroness had helped to arrange the women's visit to their home village of Fronhausen to compensate for what her Schenken ancestors had done to the Jews. Much to my dismay, the Schenken women decided not to meet with us because they did not want to be "interviewed" by survivors. Too bad. I really thought I would get to greet and shake hands with a real live Baroness.

Later on, Herbert, George and I drove to the house of Reverend Gerhard Fischer of Roth. He was a Lutheran pastor who had been living in the Village with his wife and two children for ten years. He struck me as unique to Germany; he was a soft, sensitive seminary type, fairly typical of spiritual leaders in America at that time. I was glad to see a clergyman of that sort in Germany. He showed us pictures of Roth that he had collected, and among them was a school picture of my mother taken in 1910 when she was ten. Gosh, how I would have liked to have known her. Standing behind her was her younger brother, Herman, who was then nine. Since the Reverend had been compiling artifacts and information about the history of Roth, Herbert talked to him for a while about his own research on the Jews of Roth. We then invited him to the upcoming dedication ceremony. He was delighted to be included and said he would read some psalms in German. Can you imagine: a psalm in German?!

After spending some time at Reverend Fisher's house, we drove with him to the village of Kehna where we recovered some very old prayer books that had been left behind by deported Jewish families decades earlier. I went through the religious relics, perusing them page by page, and picked out a few to use at the ceremony. I thought it quite symbolic that we would be using those prayer books at our ceremony; prayer books which had been left behind by Jews who had prayed with them all their lives, Jews who were deported and met tragic deaths.

We then paid a short visit to the village of Kirchhain, from which some of our relatives had come. After a quick lunch, we headed over to Amöneburg, an old medieval town where one of our ancestors, Hone Strauss, built a house around 1700. Hone was a progenitor of the Strauss family from which my father and his ancestors came. There we met with Dr. Schneider, a historian and geography teacher, who was involved in doing genealogical work and was hired by Herbert to help him with his research. He was an interesting man, and since he specialized in Jewish families of the area, he seemed appropriate for the task. Dr. Schneider had just finished conducting family searches for Herbert on my father's family when we met with him. He had assembled material about the family genealogy, age-old Jewish customs and the many special taxes that were imposed upon the Jews. We discussed all these matters with Dr. Schneider at some length. He pointed out the role of younger children and the lack of youth activities in the Jewish community. He also mentioned that due to his interest in Jews and their history, he had recently been on a trip to Israel. He enjoyed it so much that he was already planning another visit. I remember that hanging over the sofa in his living room was a sign which read: "Ich sitz hier weil Ich hier sitze" ("I sit here because I sit here"). Good German logic.

Dr. Schneider then treated us to a tour of the new museum of Amonenburg that he had founded some time earlier. Overall, we had a nice time with the historian and we got the chance to learn about his beliefs and opinions. While he never directly answered any questions regarding the Nazi era, I got the impression that he was not an anti-Semite like many others.

Following our visit to Amöneburg, we drove back to Roth and went to the house of Anna and Jacob Ruth. Another friend of theirs, Elisabeth, joined us. All the women claimed that they knew me, and Anne produced a school picture of me from when I was six. She was the girl standing right next to me in the picture. We reminisced about the past, mainly talking about school. At one point, Elizabeth spoke up and said some naively offensive things: "Your father was a good man. He worked hard just like us; he was not like the other Jews who cheated us in their trade." Later, she continued with, "Jews had money; we didn't. Remember the Jew Stieffel who had bought an acre of land that my relative wanted just so he could resell it to him at a profit?"

It is crazy – no one said anything against Hitler, only that there were some Jews who did bad things. They seemed to have an excuse for everything and managed to sidestep anything that might place partial guilt upon them or other Germans. In answer to questions about the fate of Toni's family they knew nothing. Lord, and these were supposed to be old friends? I found myself struggling with Herbert's optimistic belief that there was some good in some of these people.

Later that night, Herbert and I continued our conversations with the women from San Francisco. The discussion was, as usual, weird and full of complexities, both for them and for us. I had by then already given up on trying to explain anything – it was clear we were not going to see eye to eye on certain matters. Like me, these survivors endured by sheer luck (or due to some other kindly or Godly fate). The women were genuinely nice persons who, as young girls, had been severely damaged by their Holocaust experiences. Somehow, they still liked Germans, claiming that some of them had been kind to the girls when they were in Riga.

As the women told me, in December 1941 the Jews of Fronhausen were ordered to report to the nearest railroad station with no more than thirty kilos of goods. As they left, all of their acquaintances refused to intercede or talk with them. They were first sent to Kassel where their mother was berated and beaten because she had given away a sewing machine to a Gentile neighbor before leaving, rather than to the Nazi authorities. The girls never saw any of their belongings again. They then went on to sweat and labor in German factories for years in Riga. They were later dragged to work in a factory in Poland as the war was coming to a close and in the end they were liberated by the Russians. For the life of me, I could not figure out how these women found the strength to be so forgiving to these cruel German people.

Day 4, June 17: A Visit to Marburg and an Afternoon in Roth Meeting Various People from the Past

After a cup of coffee at George's house, we started off the day with a tour of Marburg. George and Anna's son, Heinz, joined us. He was a wonderfully naïve, handsome farmer's boy, thirty years of age. He truly exemplified a new generation of German who only wanted peace and goodness. We watched the rooster crow on top of the city hall; its wings did not flap as did the if a rooster fifty years earlier when I first saw it. We then visited the Landgraf's castle on top of the hill and St. Elisabeth's Church. I also made a point to visit the Jewish cemetery of Marburg. Although it was closed and fenced off, I snuck in through a hole in the fence. It appeared similar to Roth's cemetery except that it was bigger. I walked through it to pay my respects to those lying there. Somewhere in that cemetery, some of our forefathers of the Stern and Strauss families were buried, but the old tombstones were not legible so I failed to find them.

At lunchtime, George and his son did some more reading in "Platt" Deutsch, the local German dialect – it sounded very Welsh-like. We then met again with Dr. Schneider who showed us his museum. He had displays showing that the Celts were ancestors of the Germans, just like the Welsh. Later in the afternoon, George showed us a book of manuscripts of his family going back to the 1600's, and documents of the assets of his family over 200 years old. He also showed us an old school book from 1886, which contained many war stories; one was entitled the "Gute Juden" (Good Jew). I had him read it. It was about a poor farmer woman who had to borrow four marks on her last possession, a Christian Bible. The Jewess let her have the money and keep the Bible too. Humorously, I thought "Good for us!"

Once back in Roth, we returned to the Jewish cemetery. On the way to the hill, we visited Mr. Koch, an eighty year old man who moved into Toni's house after her mother and brothers were deported. I was hoping he might have some pictures of Toni's family, but he could not remember having any. His son and daughter-in-law happened to be at the house when we stopped by. They seemed sympathetic to the German-Jewish narrative. I found that the younger Germans were much easier to talk to about the fate of the Jews of the Village. The son said that he remembered how as a young boy, older boys used to throw stones and snowballs at the Jews who had remained in Roth after we left. Finally someone from the Village remembered – admitted, really – that Jews had in fact lived there. He also mentioned that he used to look forward to eating matzos that the Jews gave to his family. Oddly enough, matzo was consistently brought up by villagers with whom we talked as one of the things they liked about the Jews. The Jews gave this unleavened bread to them each year. I guess matzos taste different if you are not obligated to eat them!

Across the street from the Koch home, we engaged in conversation with the daughter of the woman who used to live next to the synagogue. She remembered Toni's mother, Bertha, coming into her store (before her deportation) at the hour when Jews were allowed out of their houses (1:00 to 2:00 in the afternoon). Jews had strict curfews back then. She recalled that Bertha brought some of her linens and other personal possessions to the store in order make a trade for some food. The woman claimed she was quite certain that even to that day, some of those items Bertha traded were still at this woman's house.

We finally made it up to the Jewish cemetery and tried to clean up and decipher the old gravestones. We succeeded on some but failed miserably on others. Neither the Hebrew nor the German could be read on some of them. A few of the old villagers came by and commented that the cemetery looked better than it had ever before. Herbert agreed that this was so and that the Jews did not take good care of the cemetery years earlier. After doing some work at the cemetery, I took a walk in the surrounding woods and then along the river Lahn as the sun was setting. I photographed the beautiful fields, the river, the dams and the old farm houses.

Strangely enough, when we returned to the Village proper, several women approached me saying that they went to school with me and remembered what a wonderful boy I was.

Humorously, I thought to myself, "I bet that they told that same thing to all the Jewish boys they encountered passing through the Village." However, I was the only one of their age who had survived.

Herbert and I had another discussion with Konrad. He said he was upset with me because last time I told him that the German people could have done something about Hitler. What an outrageous claim on my part! He could not understand that, since the consequences for speaking out meant getting shot by the Nazis. We did not argue with Konrad. We kept quiet knowing that we wanted to be very careful with this former neighbor of our family despite the fact that, in my mind, none of those people had been a part of either of our lives for over forty years.

At the end of the evening, we saw the women from San Francisco once again. They had just returned from visiting a distant relative who happened to be the product of a mixed marriage and who was now a *viehhändler* (a "cattle dealer") in the area – the trade of his ancestors. The women also found the people in Fronhausen were very warm and welcoming. They had seen their old house and they were so moved by the experience that they were unable to talk about it.

Day 5, June 18: Researching Jewish History at the Darmstadt-Hesse Archives

After a quick breakfast, we got an early start to the day and made the hour and a half drive to Darmstadt. We headed straight to the center of the city where we parked the car and went to the Hessian State Archives in Darmstadt which were only a couple of blocks away. A statue of Ludwig I stood towering above us on a high column in the center of the plaza, like a Kaiser of old. Nearby, was a statue of his son Ludwig II, sitting on a horse just like the Kaiser of the Second Reich.

Upon entering the archives, we searched through a catalog of materials about the Jews of Nieder-Ohmen, Alsfeld and Angerod. We managed to find a number of wonderful folios that included information dealing with the existence and upkeep of Jewish *mikvahs* (ritual baths), schools, and synagogues. Notable among the material we retrieved were the following: a document recording that a neighbor filed a complaint against another Jew for having emptied out the *mikvah* water onto his property; another document showing that a Jewish teacher complained that animals were being slaughtered by fellow Jews on the lower floor of his synagogue and that the stench was terrible; a number of letters from my paternal great-grandfather, Markus Roth, written to the authorities in Giessen about a disturbance in the synagogue; papers giving evidence that Markus Roth had been an elder for the Jews of Nieder-Ohmen; and some misleading inserts suggesting that another Jew, a Johann Adam Roth, had been appointed a minter of coins for Ludwig I. Regarding this last find, Herbert was sure that this was yet another forefather of ours. It turned out that the girl who had put Johann Adam Roth in the folio of the Jews of Hesse did only because she thought his name sounded Jewish. Herbert and I were disappointed that our biggest claim to fame had quickly disappeared. Before leaving the archives, we made copies of the material that we had reviewed to take back home. Unfortunately, no records of Jewish wills or probate of estates were recovered. These were documents that must have existed at some point in time but have since disappeared.

In reviewing the documents from the day, Herbert was very proud we had such important ancestors: our great-grandfather, Markus Roth, was an elder in Nieder-Ohmen, our great-grandfather, Herz Stern, was an elder in Roth, and a great-great-grandfather, a man named Max Rothschild, was an elder in Angerod. Thank God we are famous!

The day's finds led to many philosophical discussions. It seemed that the Jews clearly were allowed to practice their own religion and had their own school, *mikvah*, synagogues and judicial remedies. Yet, when Herbert and I reflected on what we remembered from life in the Village, no Jewish culture as such could be retrieved from our memory. By the 1930s, much of the Jewish learning in the Village of Roth had disappeared. But, from later conversations with Toni, she had many memories of learning Bible with her mother. We were frustrated since we simply did not know the extent of the Jewish education that the Jews of Roth received in earlier years. Suffice to say that the Jews had their own schools for many years and all of them must have been literate in Hebrew.

Day 6, June 19: Visiting Worms and Frankfurt, Uncovering the Truth of Herz Stern's Death

We drove to Worms in the morning for some sightseeing. We parked on Markplaza and walked to the *Judengasse* (meaning "Jews lane") where we found the Rashi Museum and the old restored synagogue. We watched a slide show and then took a tour of the *mikvah*, the old synagogue, and *Rashi's* room. I even got to sit in the seat in which *Rashi* supposedly sat. I was impressed with the sites. These were substantial contributions to preserving Jewish culture. We toured the rest of the museum, bought some books, and then browsed through some local shops. I bought a book on the history of the Jews of Worms from the eleventh century up until Hitler's time.

After sitting in a café for a while, we took off for Frankfurt. Our first task was to continue our search for what had happened to our grandfather, Herz. I called the Jewish cemetery in Frankfurt and set up an appointment for that afternoon with the caretaker, Mr. Horwitz. He was an interesting man. Mr. Horwitz was a Holocaust survivor from Poland whose son was currently serving in the German army. Mr. Horwitz had decided that he had wanted to live in Frankfurt and became the fulltime caretaker of the Jewish cemetery there. When Herbert and I arrived, we started looking through the ledger for a Herz Stern who we assumed had died in 1941 or 1942. No such name appeared. Mr. Horwitz assured us that if a Jewish person in Frankfurt died or was transported from there, he would definitely be on a list. He called the Jüdische Gemeinde (Jewish Community Center) to check their records. I was skeptical whether they would have anything related to Herz since they had no record of him when I visited in 1953 or when Herbert was there two years earlier.

In the meantime, we walked around and found the grave of our grandfather on our father's side, Jonas Roth, who died in 1938. I had forgotten my prayer book so I said what I remembered of the Kaddish. The cemetery was beautifully maintained. Along the sides were gravestones in memory of Jews who died at Theresienstadt.

When we got back to Mr. Horwitz's office, he informed us that he had spoken to a woman who told him she had found a record for a Herz Stern from Roth, born on March, 24, 1866. The news was terribly shocking. He had been deported to Theresienstadt on August 18, 1942 and died there on January 15, 1943. I had tears in my eyes: that poor old man. All those years we thought he had died in a hospital in Frankfurt. Suddenly, we learned that in his sickness they sent him to a ghetto to die deserted, without his family, without his friends, without anyone. After hearing the report, we drove with Mr. Horwitz to the Jüdische Gemeinde building and had them make us a copy of the record of my grandfather's death.

Later that evening I got into a discussion with Herbert as to what we would do with the marker commemorating the Holocaust victims, which bore the notation as "Frankfurt" for Herz's place of death. We called the gravestone cutter in order to bring up the issue. He said that he would have to redo the entire stone and that it would be very expensive. We would have to wait for another day to settle the matter.

Day 7, June 20: More Time Spent in and around Roth

We picked up Herbert's wife, Elsa, from the airport and drove to Nieder-Ohmen where Herbert saw people he knew. We also went to look for the house in which our father was born and our grandparents had lived. Instead, we found a parking lot where the house once stood. We then went to pay our respects to our grandmother, Lina who was buried in the Jewish cemetery there. The Burgermeister (meaning "mayor") told us the cemetery would soon be mowed in order to maintain its upkeep.

From the cemetery, we went to visit Willy Muth whose father had lived in Roth and had been a leftist. Willy was a prisoner-of-war in Russia for over five years. His two brothers were killed in World War II. Willy spoke about his recent visit to Buchenwald in East Germany. He shared the disturbing fact that the guidebook he had brought back from Buchenwald had never once mentioned that Jews had died in that concentration camp. Apparently only Communists were killed by the Nazis. What irony!

Later that afternoon I took a walk into Roth and once again

enjoyed a pleasant stroll along the river Lahn. I was still unable to overcome my discomfort with interacting with Germans. A woman who had come up to me on the street talked to me just like I had never left the place. It still just did not feel right or natural for me to interact with these people.

A bit later, I returned to the hotel. Trude Wetmore and her husband had finally arrived. She was the sole survivor of the Hochster family of Roth. Her sister, Ilse; brother, Helmuth; and their parents were deported and all perished. This trip was her first time back to her birthplace in forty five years. I took Trude and her husband for a ride back to Roth and, all things considered, she was really quite brave through it all. Quite a number of people greeted her warmly in the Village.

That night after dinner, the entire group (including Elsa, Trude and her husband, and Otto Stern and his son, Arnie) had a very nice conversation. Having been a member of the American army during the war, Otto recounted his war experiences and his confrontational return to the Village or Roth at the end of the war. He also had been the one who ordered the initial cleaning up of the Village's Jewish cemetery.

Trude had brought a letter with her that had been written by a man named Karl Stern to her older brother in 1946. Karl, who was on the train ride to Riga with the Hochsters, had survived the war. The letter described in detail the horror endured by the Jews in Riga and the deaths of so many innocent people. There was no reference to any "kind" Germans in this letter.

As I was getting ready for the big day to follow, my thoughts wandered a bit. I wondered what had changed since my first visit in 1954 when I had walked the village roads and countryside. I really could not say. I whistled German tunes back then as I did on the current trip. The fields still looked beautiful – the flowers, *mohn*, ("poppies"), *kornblumen* ("corn flowers") and daisies. The Lahn appeared smaller than I remembered it.

Day 8, June 21: Dedication and the preceding Events

The day of the dedication had finally arrived. After a brief breakfast, we all drove to Roth. I wanted to walk the road to Niederwalgern, as I had as a child, but Otto, who also wanted to go to Niederwalgern, preferred to drive on this stone-paved road. We took the car and drove to the old railroad station in Niederwalgern and Otto explained to me that my father once had a small warehouse next to the station. I had completely forgotten about that.

Otto's grandfather and my grandfather were first cousins and interestingly, each was named Herz Stern. Otto and I were not only second cousins but also very close friends. In fact, he tells the story that he was one of the first people to reach my mother's bedside when I was born. He says he was returning to the village with his father when he heard that my father, Markus, had a new son. He jumped down from the wagon, ran up the stairs before anyone could stop him, and ran into the room in which my mother was resting with me, where children were not allowed. Thus my friendship with him began at my birth and continues to this day.

Otto and I then drove to an old farmhouse. There, we talked to an old woman who remembered me and my father and also Otto's grandfather, Herz Stern. She even remembered Herz's birthday was the first of April. Others came by and referred to Herz Stern as a "*Hofude*," (meaning "court Jew") apparently a term for the village's Jewish peddler. This did not seem to bother Otto much but it really irked me. The Hofude was the local Jew given the right to sell his wares to the non-Jews in a certain area, which I suppose at the time would have been a coveted position. Still, in my opinion, referring to Jews by this term was derogatory and just another inadvertent slights toward the Jews.

Afterwards, we started getting ready for the ceremony. I met with the video operator and helped set up his camera. We took pictures of the Village and then drove through Roth to photograph our house, Toni's family's house, Otto's house, and other relevant sites in the Village.

While we were photographing around the Village, we bumped into a group of young Germans (not from Roth) who happened to be in the area. We spoke with them briefly and some of them were really quite genuine in their sympathy. One in particular, a pretty young girl on her bike, was delightful. She could not understand why the Villagers did not hide the Jews. "Not even one was saved?" she inquired. "No," I said, "not even one."

We then proceeded to photograph the small building which

used to be the Village synagogue. By then it had deteriorated into quite a shabby condition and was being used as a grain warehouse. Amazingly, the white stars on the blue canvas on the inside ceiling were still visible; I remembered them from when I was young. Also, if one looked closely, some Hebrew letters written on the walls of the synagogue were still apparent. One of the psalms written on the walls in Hebrew was from Psalm 26, verse 8. It read, translated to English, as follows:

> "Oh, Lord, I love thy abode
> the place where thy glory dwelleth!"

The psalms were very important for my ancestors since they held special spiritual and religious significance in the Jewish tradition. We found psalms in many of the prayer books that had been left behind by those who were deported. Being inside the synagogue was chilling. Our synagogue, built over one hundred years earlier, was still standing because the Nazis refrained from burning it down during Kristallnacht in November 1938. Apparently, they had feared that it might start a fire that could spread to the surrounding buildings. I figured that the synagogue building would, in all probability, remain in its current state until it fell down by itself. I was convinced that the villagers themselves would do nothing to make it a holy shrine once more, and I figured that it was probably against German law for them to tear it down. And what motivation did Herbert and I have to restore it? For whom would we be doing such a thing? For what? It seemed quite clear that no Jews intended to move back to Roth. After all this was not Worms. Little did I know at that time, that about a decade later, renovations on the synagogue would in fact begin, not by any Jew, but by a group of young non-Jewish residents of the Village.

After the picture-taking, we headed over to the cemetery where we met the rest of the participants in the ceremony. Everyone was a bit tense and emotional. There were many people in attendance, including a great number of the villagers. A group from the Association for Christian-Jewish Cooperation in Marburg was also there. The camera was set up and Herbert gave the introduction. His speech included the following eulogy:

> We are the last Jews of Roth, once expelled – saved – we stand here to commemorate those who perished more than forty years ago. We seek to remember them by erecting this tablet so that later generations will know that they, our parents, sisters, brothers and friends were from Roth, and that they were murdered only because they were Jews.
>
> One learns how to accept in age – but we will not forget. Time heals the wounds – but the scars remain as a constant reminder of this most dastardly deed.
>
> In this village, which they loved, we record their names – for eternal remembrance.

JOSEPH BERGENSTEIN	HERMANN HOCHSTER
KLARA BERGENSTEIN	BERTHA HOCHSTER
HEINZ BERGENSTEIN	ILSE HOCHSTER
KURT BERGENSTEIN	HELMUTH HOCHSTER

GERTRUDE NATHAN	BERTHA STERN
PAUL INE NATHAN	LOUIS STERN
ZILLY NATHAN	HUGO STERN

HERZ STERN

I spoke next and for some reason my English changed to German as I began speaking about my grandfather. I have translated my speech back into English:

> Our mother Selma Stern died here on February 28, 1934, and is buried here. Our mother's father does not lie here. We thought that he had died in Frankfurt. But this week we discovered that he had been deported to Theresienstadt in 1942, and died there on January 15, 1943. He had written us from Frankfurt in 1941 that he was sick and had been in a hospital. For that reason we thought he had died there, but we were mistaken. Herz Stern represents the tragedy that befell our families. He was a good man. His father and fathers before him lived in this village. His son, Herman, was killed in 1917 at the age of seventeen while fighting for the German army. Herz's daughter, my mother, lies here. He was murdered in his old age by the Nazis. We remember him today and pray that, as we say in English, 'Never Again.'

Others spoke after me. Reverend Fischer, whom we had invited a few days prior, spoke beautifully:

> I begin with the words Shema Israel from the five books of Moses. 'Hear, O' Israel: The Lord is our God, the Lord is One. You shall love the Lord your God with all your heart, with all your strength, with all your being.' This word has a long history, a history that you probably understand better than is possible for us. This story begins over 2,500 years ago with Moses and the

> people of Israel and reaches down to us over Auschwitz. The belief in the One God requires the love of One God. Moses taught the people that if you obey your God, then you will live. It is for this reason, that this prayer was often said in times of danger – like in Auschwitz, a place of great danger – that made clear the wickedness present in the world. This affirmation to pray, 'Hear, O' Israel: The Lord is our God,' contrasts sharply with the wickedness of man. It points to the strife and struggle of a world in which God's word was not heard.
>
> We thank you, that in this place, we can commemorate with you your dead. I see it as a sign of Shalom, of peace, that comes from God. We want to seize this hand, and with you, this history – which for you began here in Roth – and for us continues here. I thank you for this hand of peace which you have offered us. Again thanks.

Reverend Fischer concluded by saying he would preach about all this in his upcoming Sunday sermon in the church in Roth. The Reverend finished his sermon by reading the traditional Psalm 23 in German. He was really very magnificent.

The Mayor of Roth then placed a wreath at the foot of the memorial and said:

> In the name of the Village, Roth, and its citizens I lay down this wreath in memory of the Jewish fellow-citizens who lived here in Roth, and who died here. But especially in memory of those fellow-citizens who under bitter circumstances were forced to leave their homes, and those who were expelled and lost their lives. I thank Mr. Roth – the brothers Roth – for the erection of this memorial since it will aid us to remember that the past always remains and should never be forgotten. This memorial shall be a warning in the best sense.

The service concluded with a sermon by Rabbi Weiss, the

chanting of traditional Hebrew prayers for the dead, and the recital of the Kaddish prayer, both in German and in Aramaic.

Herbert then attempted to summarize the whole ceremony with these words:

> It is not easy for me in German to find the right words to say, what is in my heart – but I will try. If we all heard what Reverend Fisher said, and if we all could believe and live what he said here, then perhaps the fate of these people had a meaning. Then perhaps, one can say, it was worth it, namely, a man goes through life and asks often: 'Why, what is it that we leave behind?' So if, a better comprehension, a better man, a better understanding of other peoples, other religions, other races, of other countries can come from such a fate, then perhaps their death had a meaning.

I was quite emotional throughout the ceremony. My heart was beating rapidly and I was very sensitive to it all. Among the people at the ceremony appeared Else Wenz, my old nursemaid who had taken care of me when I was a youngster in Roth. I had no feeling for her at all nor did I have any desire to try to open up to her. She said she was there with me when my mother died and when my grandmother died. Maybe she was. However, I had no memory of her ever expressing any sympathy for what had happened to me and my family.

Others also approached me to talk with me during this time. I became overwhelmed and decided I'd had enough. I drove off with Rabbi Weiss through the Village and along the way we noticed Konrad standing in front of his house. We stopped and had a chat with him. Konrad was amazed by Rabbi Weiss's role as an army Chaplin and he could not believe that such an important rabbi was also involved with American non-Jewish soldiers.

I also had an interesting encounter with a gentleman from the Marburg Christian Jewish Society. He was very agitated when telling me that none of the villages of Hesse had done anything to memorialize their Jewish past. He said that in other parts of Germany, towns and villages were honoring their Jewish dead, but not in that area. He also thought it was scandalous that we, not the Village, had to pay for the memorial tablet.

That evening, we ate supper at the hotel and then went back to George's for dessert. No matter what, in Germany one must eat well. I was glad the day was over, though. The long day was one filled with intense emotion and left me empty. My thoughts drifted and I started to focus on the missing members of my family who were still with us when we lived in Roth – my father, my sister, my grandfather and my step-mother – and what had happened to them after we left Germany. Of the four, only Toni was still alive at the time of this trip.

Day 9, June 22: Departing events post Memorial

As was my routine, after breakfast I once again spoke with the women from San Francisco. They came up to me to thank me and apologized for not having been able to successfully arrange the meeting with the Schencken Baroness. Truth be told, I think I did in fact see the Schencken in the hotel hallway a few days prior when I was going to my room. The women said that the Baroness' daughter was too upset to see us and that she placed all blame on her family for all that happened to the Jews. The old Baroness was apparently very old. Her husband was the ambassador to Japan for Hitler.

There were grades of Schencken living in the Burgs (which are small castles) – higher Burgs, middle Burgs and lower Burgs (and *Hamburgers*) and there were even rivalries between these various Burgs. The Baroness' husband was Schenck *von* Fronhausen, meaning he was Schenck *from* Fronhausen. One of his relatives was Schenck "zu" Schweinsberg meaning Schenck *connected with* Schweinsberg, which was a larger village nearby. If I had been a descendant of a Teutonic Knight I might have been known as "*Walter von und zu Roth.*"

Afterwards, we went with George to a press conference with a reporter from the *Oberhessische Zeitung*. The reporter was a neophyte who was substituting for the regular Mr. Schmitz with whom we had met earlier. He was really an unemployed teacher who knew little about the whole Jewish business. For example, he thought George was a Jew since his name sounded like a Jewish name. We reviewed our story for him and then we all went with him back up to the cemetery to take some pictures there.

After that we packed up and drove off to Marburg. I took a ride up to the Schloss (meaning "castle") with Herbert and his wife, and then walked to a nice restaurant overlooking the city where I had eaten lunch two years earlier. On the way to our final destination, the Frankfort Airport, we drove to Bad Nauheim, an old sprawling spa with beautiful gardens, birds, swans, and pigeons. The only visitors seemed to be very old people.

Day 10, June 23: Final Thoughts and Reflections

There are some things that never change. When you go back in time to your early years, you can recreate the tension quickly. You can recreate it later too; but it helps to understand how it arose. But strangest of all is the human mind which recalls the saddest memories even after all these years, and then forgets things more joyful. The death of my mother, Selma, when I was five was a hurt lasting a lifetime, compounded by the tragedy of the Jews of Roth that followed. Yet, the persons who made it possible for us to come to the United States were my father and the relatives of my step-mother, Toni, who over the years became the lifeline of our family. As I concluded this trip in 1984, my thoughts were overwhelmed memories of the lives of both my father and Toni.

9

2003 VISIT: INTRODUCING THE THIRD GENERATION

In the summer of 2003, Chaya and I embarked on a trip with our daughter, Judy, her husband, Steve Zeldes, and their two children, Miko and Tema. The purpose of this trip was to introduce two of our grandchildren to the history of their grandparents in Italy and Germany. This would be the first visit by members of the third generation Roth since our family was uprooted from Germany. This trip and later, a follow-up 2011 trip were very significant in this respect.

We landed in Milan, Italy, and visited many of the places in which Chaya, her sister, and her mother had sought refuge from the Nazis during the years 1943 and 1944. We spent a week in northern Italy and we were successful in locating some of the people who helped save Chaya's family, including the priest, Don

Francesco Brondello, who was later awarded by Yad Vashem the title of "Righteous among the Nations." I leave this story to Chaya who has written a brilliant book about the entire tale called *The Fate of Holocaust Memories*.

We left Italy driving for a few lovely days through the Alps, Switzerland, and then into Germany itself. We arrived in Roth and met with Rabbi Amnon Orbach who lives in Marburg. He has also spent some of his time working with the Roth community. We also met with Annegret Wenz Haubfleisch and Gabi Schmitt who were both very involved in facilitating the activities relating to the restoration of the synagogue in Roth, which occurred in 1998. They were among the founding members of the *Arbeitskreis Landsynogogue* Roth. An *Arbeitskreis* is a working group or a rather informal association of people with a common goal. Our next visit to Roth, which would be in 2011, would have a particular emphasis on matters relating to the synagogue, its restoration, and the people who worked to restore it. I write about that most recent trip in the following chapter.

Annegret and Gabi took us on excursions to the Jewish cemetery and introduced Miko and Tema to many interesting places in the area. They picked raspberries and took hikes along the river Lahn which the children loved. We had coffee and cake at Annegret's mother's house and we noted that her cakes evoked memories of the ones baked by my stepmother, Toni. Later that evening we had a nice Shabbat dinner with Annegret and Rabbi Orbach.

On Sunday we went to Marburg with Laurence Bryant from Roth, a member and now associate chair of the Arbeitskreis, who gave us a wonderful tour of the city. She also gave us a book containing various stories concerning Roth's history. We saw many historically significant sites in Marburg including old churches. Among these churches was St. Elisabeth Church and the residence in which the Grimm brothers lived.

On Monday we went to visit an elderly lady, A. Rut, who claimed she had been a classmate and "girlfriend" of mine. She even had a picture to prove it! She had not changed much since the last time I saw her, which was in 1984. At the time of this writing, we were still in touch and corresponded at least once a year during the holiday season.

We also had the fortunate opportunity to attend a meeting held in the synagogue. The old desecrated synagogue had been restored and solemnly opened in 1998. Annegret Wenz-Haubfleisch, current chair of the Arbeitskreis, tells the history of the synagogue restoration as follows:

> In 1938 the Jewish community had to pay for the cleaning up of the synagogue. Shortly afterwards, in February 1939, they were forced to sell the synagogue. It was sold to the neighboring cabinet maker Paul Hormel. The mikvah and the yard were sold to the neighboring farmer, Konrad Eidam. Years later Paul Hormel sold the synagogue to Johannes Eidam, Konrad's son, who then stored his grain in it. In order to be restored, Johannes Eidam sold it to the community of Weimar. From the community, a little later, the court of Marburg took it. It is still in the possession of the county. The Artbeitskreis signed a contract

> with the county in 1998 by which it received the sole responsibility for the cultural and educational work in the synagogue. (Personal Correspondence, 2012)

Annegret, a historian and associate director of the State Archives in Marburg, wrote a booklet in 2011 entitled, *A Short History of the Jews of Roth and Their Synagogue*. There she explains that since the 1980s, a group of local citizens wanted the synagogue to be restored and memorialized, to become a place of learning and of cultural activities. From 1993 to 1995, the exterior was restored, and in 1997, the interior. On March 10, 1998, it was solemnly opened to the public. Many survivors, their children and grandchildren from the United States attended the momentous ceremony. In May 1998, the Arbeitskreis Landsynagoge Roth and the county of Marburg-Biedenkopf signed a contract which became the basis of the Arbeitskreis' current work in the synagogue.

During the summer, the synagogue is regularly open on Sundays; there is a cultural program with a variety of activities. These activities include pedagogical work with children and students from nearby schools. The Arbeitskreis also plays an important role in the upkeep and maintenance of the Jewish cemetery where my mother is buried.

At the meeting, a number of members of the A*rbeitskreis* spoke about the history of the Jews of Roth. I also spoke and recounted for the audience my personal history – that of my family – particularly focusing on my mother, her brother, grandmother

Emma, and the tragedy of my beloved grandfather, Herz Stern. When the gathering ended I noted that my grandson Miko came running out of the synagogue and accosted his mother saying, “Why didn’t you ever tell us what had happened in Germany to our family?!” Interestingly enough, a reporter for a local newspaper overheard Miko’s protests and took the initiative to talk to Miko. We were told that an article about this interview later appeared in the local paper.

At the end of the trip, we drove to Frankfurt, and from there took a flight back home. While the trip in Germany was briefer than the more extensive visit to Italy, it was a very meaningful way for us to introduce members of the third generation (our grandchildren) to Roth. It was exciting for them to get glimpses of the history their grandparents and their ancestors who had lived and perished in Germany.

10

2011 VISIT

We arrived in Frankfurt, Germany on the morning of June 18th, 2011 on a direct flight from Chicago. Our group consisted of me, Chaya, Miriam and her husband Mark Raider, and their children Jonah, Emma, and Talia. We would be joined by the rest of the Roth clan two days later.

We drove from the airport to the city of Marburg, home of Marburg University, founded in 1527 as the first Protestant university in Germany. Philosophers Hermann Cohen and Martin Heidegger taught there. Hannah Arendt and Leo Strauss, both of whom had left Germany prior to World War II and subsequently became professors at the University of Chicago, studied at Marburg University as well.

In the afternoon, Annegret Wenz Haubfleisch, leader of the Arbeitskreis Landsynagoge Roth, came to our hotel. After warm embraces, we proceeded by car caravan (her Volkswagen, our rented Mercedes) to the village of Roth.

Our first stop in Roth was at the former home of my stepmother, Toni. She had lived there with her mother Bertha and her brothers Hugo and Louis. All but Toni were kept confined there until 1942, when they were deported to Theresienstadt. The house was purchased by a Mr. Koch and is now owned by his grandson, Marco Koch.

In front of the house were *stolpersteine* – "stumbling stones." A *stolpersteine* is a Holocaust memorial stone erected to commemorate those German Jews who perished during the War. A concrete block is covered with a sheet of brass. Stamped in the brass is the individual's name, year of birth, and the person's fate, as well as the dates of deportation and death, if known. These stones are then laid flush with the pavement or sidewalk in front of the last residence of a Holocaust victim. The wording begins, *Hier Wohnte* – "here lived."

And indeed, here had lived Toni's family who never made it out of Germany. The house which Mr. Koch purchased was never supposed to have been built. In an interview I conducted with my stepmother, Toni, in November 1988, she revealed to me that when her father, Mannes, decided to build this house in 1929, he and the family were advised by a stranger passing through the Village not to do so. This person believed that the Jews were all going to be thrown out of Germany. Little did any of us know at the time how true that would be. In fact, in Toni's case, her mother and brothers were not even extradited or driven out of the country; they were murdered without any chance to flee.

Seeing that house reminded me so much of Toni's years growing up in Roth. She was born to Mannes and Bertha Stern on July 21, 1898. Toni was the youngest of three: Louis was born in 1894 and Hugo in 1896. Her father, Mannes, owned a business with his brother selling dry goods.

Returning to the matter of the *stolpersteine*, these memorial stones are now visible in a number of cities and towns around Germany. The ones I mention are the only markers of this kind in the Village of Roth. I think the Kochs' attitude of publicly recognizing that they are living in a house of murdered Jews is unique in the Village.

In contrast, the present owner of my grandfather's and father's house has refused to let our family enter. He had repainted the outside a bleak gray, obliterating the inscriptions: "1774" – the year the house was built – and the quotation from Psalm 41. He also destroyed the garden and surrounded the house with a high wooden fence. I must say that I was quite upset to find the house so mistreated. We were all immensely disappointed to see such disrespect. It seems the villagers did not put up much of a protest, either.

We then walked to the restored synagogue. Unfortunately, the synagogue was devoid of the essential ritual and communal objects which once sanctified this Jewish place of worship. There was no longer a Holy Ark or Eternal Light. The benches and other interior features were also lacking. The interior of the building had instead been transformed into a museum. The women's balcony had been restored, but in a more modern style. On the floor there was a symbolically broken ceramic Star of David made by one of the *Arbeitskreis* leaders, Gabi Schmitt.

A glass case contained ritual and ceremonial objects. On one wall there were painted portraits by the artist Marlis Glaser. Annegret writes:

> On the vault of the synagogue, there was wallpaper painted in a beautifully blue color, covered with all kinds of stars and also a bright sun, which is now almost destroyed. It was Gabi Schmitt's idea to have the grandchildren of the survivors add new stars to the ceiling. The first grandchild who did this was Katelin Stern (granddaughter of Otto Stern) in 2008, on the tenth anniversary of the opening of the synagogue. It is a symbolic act of reconciliation, but we do not want to restore the pattern of stars on the original ceiling.

Each of our grandchildren also added to the firmament by painting a star. Our children also painted stars at the end of the trip.

The next afternoon, Annegret led us on a short drive to the cemetery. She had enlarged a map of all of the graves and had marked the ones related to our family history. We viewed the graves of the Roth/Stern family, which includes my mother, Selma, my grandmother, Emma, and a stone which notes that the space had been reserved for my grandfather, Herz Stern. In another part of the cemetery, we stopped at the gravestones of our other ancestors. Annegret pointed out that our family history has deep roots in Roth.

Emma, like the other grandchildren, was quite affected by the experience. Although she had been the "unofficial" Roth photographer for the excursion to the cemetery, she disappeared for a while, wandering on her own. We later found her sitting in a luscious field of grain contemplating the fate of our ancestors.

We met up with Ari, his wife Katie, and daughter Sophie and set out for Berlin, our next stop. It was a five hour drive from Marburg. Our Mercedes Super Van was followed by our son Ari's rented BMW. Our journey had one telling incident en route that illustrates the state of the German character. When we returned to our van after a brief "pit stop," we were surrounded by a number of tall, uniformed German soldiers. Their leader was not unfriendly, but he was rigid and unyielding. It appeared that one of the young soldiers claimed that we had caused a scratch on their military vehicle when the front door of the van was opened. It appeared to us that it was only a little scratch, and we were not convinced that we had caused it. The leader of the German soldiers had already called the military police to report it, and we were told that we could not move until the police arrived. We had someone call the local police for us, as we would have done in America. After we handed over our insurance information, we drove off with a most unpleasant taste of the intransigence and rigidity of the German mentality. The whole fiasco lasted over two hours.

We finally arrived in Berlin and settled in at the elegant Hilton Hotel. We reunited with Judy, Steve, Miko and Tema. We missed Isabel, Ari and Katie's oldest child, who was beginning her illustrious teaching career in California.

The next afternoon we went to Adas Yisroel cemetery, where Chaya's father, Aaron Jacob Horowitz, was buried after he was beaten to death in KZ Sachsenhausen in 1939. Chaya's great-grandfather, Isaac Kupferstock, was buried next to him in 1940.

We then drove to Chaya's family's former residence, an apartment on Alte Schonhauser Strasse. Although that apartment was being repainted and could not be entered, Chaya was invited in by the occupants of a similar unit in the building. The lady who lived there showed us all the rooms and Chaya remembered that behind the dining room was situated a very small kitchen – the lady reaffirmed that Chaya was correct.

Next, we went to the Muntz Strasse, where Chaya's great-grandfather, a Hassidic rabbi, had a little *shul* (known as a *shtibl*) and where his family lived. Chaya tells his story in her book. As we climbed to the second floor where Chaya thought the *shul* was located, we met a young man who was a movie producer. He was very interested in our search, and he then told me of his story and his role as a film maker. He gave us a DVD of a film he had made about a tragic event during the Holocaust.

The next day, we drove to KZ Sachsenhausen (a notorious Nazi concentration camp), now a museum. Sylvia, a guide whom we had met earlier, joined us. The camp has been "sanitized," and has a modern wall surrounding all of it. We spent nearly six hours there, learning of the history of this concentration camp, seeing some of its cells, and viewing a documentary film about the cruelty perpetrated there. At one point, our group sat in a large circle next to the Appel Platz to discuss what we had seen. Chaya spoke movingly to us about the life of her father which brutally ended with his murder at the camp. The group was deeply affected.

The camp, which is right next to the village of Oranienburg, imprisoned tens of thousands of Jews (amongst other political prisoners) and sent many more to their death. The thousands of inhabitants of the nearby village could see what was going on, yet they all sat idly and did nothing to stop the Nazis. We left in a somber mood, eager to depart from the awful place.

We drove back to Marburg, and later that evening to Roth for the Arbeitskreis' Fifteenth Anniversary Celebration. Before the celebration, our family held a *Kabbalat Shabbat* (welcoming the Sabbath) service in the synagogue, bringing the spirit of prayer into the building. At the celebration in the synagogue, I was among several people who were asked to speak. I praised the forty-member *kreis* for the work they have done to date, and I encouraged them to pursue their objective of transmitting the lessons of the Holocaust to future generations. I also stressed the need for the people of the village to admit what had happened in Germany. We then had a very well-prepared dinner in a barn, in a spirit of comradeship.

On Sunday we returned to the synagogue for a klezmer band concert by three women from Frankfurt. The audience enjoyed it very much and joined in a sing-along and dancing. Emma particularly enjoyed herself with her new-found friend of the same age from Roth, Salome. It was a very meaningful culmination to our visit to have Emma and Salome, members of the third generation of Jews and Germans, become good friends, with plans to correspond and exchange visits – a good omen for future possibilities.

PART II:

PHOTOS

Markus (far right) with immediate family

Markus (top left) and Nieder-Omen Family

Berta

Hugo

Selma

Walter and Grandpa Herz

Grandpa Herz

Herbert and Irene on motorcycle in Roth, Germany

Walter (third from right in middle row)with grade school class in Germany

New York, Liner on which Walter and family arrived in America

Roth Synagogue exterior, prior to restoration

Interior of Roth Synagogue, after restoration began

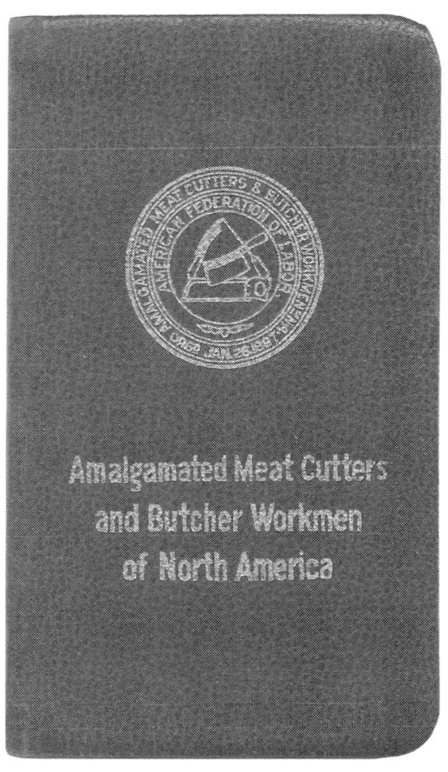

Markus' Amalgamated Meat Cutters and Buctcher Workmen Union Member Book

Cover (above), Registration page (opposite page top), Dues stamps (opposite page bottom)

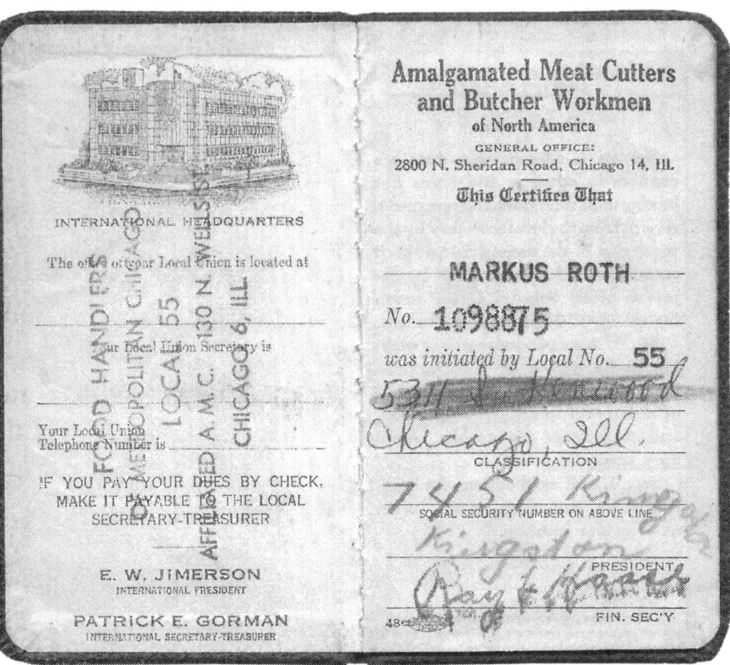

INTERNATIONAL HEADQUARTERS

The office of your Local Union is located at

Your Local Union Secretary is

Your Local Union Telephone Number is

IF YOU PAY YOUR DUES BY CHECK, MAKE IT PAYABLE TO THE LOCAL SECRETARY-TREASURER

FOOD HANDLERS OF METROPOLITAN CHICAGO
LOCAL 55
AFFILIATED A.M.C. 130 N. WELLS ST.
CHICAGO 6, ILL.

E. W. JIMERSON
INTERNATIONAL PRESIDENT

PATRICK E. GORMAN
INTERNATIONAL SECRETARY-TREASURER

Amalgamated Meat Cutters and Butcher Workmen
of North America
GENERAL OFFICE:
2800 N. Sheridan Road, Chicago 14, Ill.

This Certifies That

MARKUS ROTH

No. 1098875

was initiated by Local No. 55

5311 S. Kenwood
Chicago, Ill.

CLASSIFICATION

7451 Kingston

SOCIAL SECURITY NUMBER ON ABOVE LINE

Kingston

PRESIDENT

FIN. SEC'Y

ARTICLE VII

Suspensions

Section 1. Membership dues are payable in advance and those not having paid their dues and received a receipt from the local secretary by the tenth day of the second month shall stand suspended, and shall be deprived of all benefits of the union for six months after reinstatement.

Sec. 3. A suspended member wishing to be reinstated must accompany his application with full amount of arrears up to date of suspension, and such other fee as the Union may prescribe.

Sec. 4. All applications for reinstatement must be voted upon at a regular meeting.

A. M. C. & B. W. OF N. A.

MONTHLY DUES
1956

January	April
1-11-56 $4.00	PAY YOUR DUES PROMPTLY OR YOU LOSE YOUR DEATH BENEFIT!
	May REMEMBER YOUR DUES ARE PAYABLE IN ADVANCE!
	June PAY YOUR DUES PROMPTLY OR YOU LOSE YOUR DEATH BENEFIT!

Markus and Toni, taken in Chicago

Herbert's wedding weekend:
Left to Right, beginning at top: Helen, Herbert, Elsa, Walter, Markus, Toni, Irene

Walter's trip to Germany in 2011 included all of his children and grandchildren with the exception of his granddaughter Isabel, who was preparing for Teach for America

Left to Right:

Katie | Ari | Chaya | Walter | Miko | Jonah | Emma | Steve

| Sophie | Tema | Miriam | Judy

| Talia

Walter and Granddaughter Isabel

Salome's Visit to the USA to see Emma
Left to right, beginning at top:
Emma, Chaya, Walter, Mark, Miriam,
Talia, Salome

Herbert, Helen and Walter

PART III:

LETTERS FROM ROTH

11

SUPPLEMENTAL LETTERS

After Toni, my stepmother, passed away at the age of ninety nine in a self-help-home in Chicago, I found among her belongings a steel safety deposit box which contained many of her valuables and family artifacts. These included a batch of letters mailed from Germany, which were from Toni's mother Berta, brothers Louis and Hugo, as well as a few letters from my grandfather, Herz Stern. My family had known of these letters, but we were surprised to find that Toni had kept each and every one of them. Since the letters were written in a German handwriting in style that was of an older era, none of my immediate family could translate the letters. I turned to one of my older relatives, Marga Bachenheimer, originally from a village near Roth, who was able to read and understand the letters. However, after reading only a few, she broke down crying due to the contents and was unable to continue.

I turned the letters over to my brother, Herbert, who made

contact with a German translator. The translator transcribed the script from the letters into typed font and returned them to us in fully legible German. From there, Herbert translated some of the letters himself into English and used a small portion of the letters within his book, History of the Jews of Roth (private printing). The typed transcript was eventually given to my sister Helen and her husband, Lowell Dittmer. Lowell, a professor of Asian history at Berkeley who happens to be fluent in German, graciously volunteered to translate the letters into English.

With each letter I have taken some liberties, editing portions that I felt were either vague in reference or repetitive. The deleted portions mostly refer to names of people who were not from the village of Roth - many were distant relatives or German Jewish acquaintances but had no connection with my family in Chicago. Additionally, I have omitted a few letters in their entirety because they were repetitious. Each letter from Berta also contained a note at the end from Hugo and Louis. As time passed they wrote less and less and thus some of their notes are not included.

In reading through these letters, it's important to note that Berta, Hugo and Lewis, with whom we were in almost contact bi-weekly, never made mention of non-Jewish Germans in town. Their main focus was constant references to obtaining travel papers, otherwise referred to as affidavits or guarantees, that would secure their departure from Germany.

As a boy of about ten when these letters started to arrive, I have some memory of their existence. However I didn't remember their contents, nor did my father and Toni discuss with me the situation my family in Roth was facing. From the context of the letters, I know my family in Roth was kept up to date on me and my siblings and I even remember including a couple of my own notes in Toni's letters to Germany. The last communication we had from my family in Roth was a Red Cross Telegram sent by Berta congratulating me on my becoming Bar Mitzvah in April 1942 (included).

Letter 1, December 17, 1938

My family, and me, my brother Herbert, my father Markus, sister Irene, and my stepmother Toni, at the time secretly pregnant with my sister Helen, arrived in Chicago via New York in June, 1938. This is the first letter from Germany, prior to our arrival in the US that Toni kept. In looking at this first letter versus later letters, there is no urgency involving the papers necessary for leaving Germany as conveyed by Berta. The letter maintains a casual tone, and it's obvious that there were prior communications as this letter references my cousin Julius' hardships finding a job in the US, which were apparently exacerbated by his inability to speak English.

Additionally it's important to note that other Jews from the village were attempting to leave for not only the US, but also other foreign countries. In this letter, Holland is mentioned and later letters also make reference to England, South America, Africa and even China. Also of note is a reference to the Jews being able to leave their homes and travel in the community - it appears they were not completely confined to their residences at this time. This is supported by Berta's interactions with the Bluems, our neighbors from Roth. Most importantly, this letter is written prior to the outbreak of the war.

Roth, December 17, 1938

Meine Lieben,

Yesterday morning received your letter and were delighted to discover things are going well with you; also we are, thank God, healthy. The papers we have all received, as I already wrote to you, this misses the main point Joseph has not yet gotten his guarantee perhaps it will come in the course of the week. Heinz Kurt, as well as Bluem's girl and Helmut have registered for Holland and very probably will be gone shortly. Heinz was gone again Friday; we were with them the other evening. Aunt Dina appears to have changed completely, she goes out so little here and only if she only can she wants to. I am very sorry that Julius does not have work yet; perhaps the children could speak English with him. If you can teach a bear to dance it should be possible to teach Julius to speak English. Friday I usually fill the oven in the living room with briquettes, then it goes pretty well, but since yesterday we had a cold wave that was really hard to take and although I stoked up the fire, the windows still froze to the top. How is it with you, do you also have such cold spells? Nothing else to report. For today I send you hearty greetings and kisses,

Your

Berta

Letter 2, January 14, 1939

This letter is full of optimism in regards to leaving Germany. I have been unable to figure out whether the references to the kitchen table and white suits and gloves are literal, or some sort of code. There is a possibility that it is both literal and code as families departing Germany could only bring one "lift", or large container, of possessions. Many times valuables would be hidden in the objects in the lift; for example my father hid some cash in the bottom of a coffee grinder which passed by German inspection with no incident.

In this second letter my family indicates that they have numbers assigned by the American consulate in Stuttgart to leave the country. Note they had their #s in 1939, and never made it out by 1942.

Roth, Jan 14, 1939

Meine Lieben!

Your letter of Dec 24 arrived on Tuesday evening you can imagine how we waited for it. Today your January 1 letter came. Were glad to see you all well we are all healthy as well thank God. Dear Toni you have written telling us what furniture we should bring with us, should we not bring a kitchen table? Shouldn't Hugo and Louis also bring white gloves or what does one wear with white suits?

With the Bluems their travel doesn't go very fast, it all takes such a long time. Mr. Bluem was in Frankfurt on Sunday and wanted to go to the English Consulate on Monday but he was so late in the queue he didn't get back until Tuesday evening. What he wanted there I don't know, nor do I know whether he made another application. Dear Markus you ask whether Heinz cannot yet come over there, he must wait until his number comes up, so goes it with us as well, we still have a few hundred to go. Dear Hermann you played cards over the holidays, did you make any monies from this? I have nothing more to report. Hope you are all well and receive hearty greetings and kisses from

Your

Berta

Meine Lieben!

Hopefully it goes well for you all, which thank God I can report for us. Dear Julius I am delighted that Otto on Christmas received something, how is it with Herbert did he receive something also. Now to you dear Walter, I was delighted by your lines and could also read them, only the word "movie" did I not know what it means, write it to me again. Dear Otto I was delighted to see your hand signature once again. Dear Markus you ask when Hermann Bluem plans to leave, with him I think it depends not on when he takes the time, authorization has not yet come from Africa, I can only assume because of lack of space. Please receive from us the best greetings.

Your, Hugo

Letter 3, January 21, 1939

As Toni and my father feared that they would not be able to enter the US with her pregnant, they kept her pregnancy a secret both in Germany and the US for as long as possible. The letter below is the first response from Germany after Toni broke the news to her mother that she had given birth to my sister, Helen.

Roth January 21, 1939

Meine Lieben!

I received your letter today; I cannot describe how delighted and surprised we were. I am happy that you dear Toni are in such fine shape and that the child is also healthy. Receive my heartiest congratulations I will hope that my little grandchild will grow up to your and our joy. That the child weighed five pounds is yet enough. Bluem's little Irma weighed only three pounds at the time and has nonetheless grown so big. I would be very happy to be with you already, but what can I say I would rather be with you today than tomorrow to see my little grandchild. The loved ones write Helen is such a beautiful child so I am doubly excited to see her. Dear Markus that is very pleasant you are there, you need not miss anything. That you, dear Walter, do not visit your little sister I find very unjust; one must adjust to everything. To you my dear ones I thank heartily for your congratulations you cannot imagine how surprised we all were and how overjoyed now I must think of something pretty can bring with me for the grandchild or even better if you write me what to bring. I have not yet heard from my sister Dina very likely she wanted to send congratulations and papers together. The Bluem's Trude is off to Marburg to help her Aunt she will shortly leave for England also Frau Simon Kaiser goes with her, her husband is already there. In the past week we had high water, it was not in the village but around it, it has not been so high for twenty years. Now we have the most beautiful spring weather that means mild rains occasionally as usual. In conclusion I want to inquire about your health, with us, thank God, we can report only the best health. In the hope that your letters arrive here punctually I send hearty greetings and kisses

Your

Berta

In the left margin (written by Berta):

Please write to me what we should bring with us that is really practical, you will know what I mean. What should Hugo and Louis buy for gloves?

Letter 4, March 26, 1939

This set of letters comes from my mother's father, Herz. He went to live in Frankfurt with my father's sister Jenny after my immediate family left Roth. My father and Jenny had two other siblings, Mortiz, who went to England, and Leopold who went to New York in 1936. Leopold is my uncle who did not offer to put up my family upon our arrival in New York.

Frankfurt, March 26, 1939

Meine Lieben Alle!

With joy I received your letter of March 4 and learned therefrom that you are all doing well, as I can say of myself as well. For your hearty congratulations on my birthday I say to you all my heartiest thanks. I think that the time will soon come when I can do the same when I am with you, this is the only wish that I still have. Dear Markus, Lina from Rueddingshausen who is still here, also has received a guarantee from America and has the number 10000, but from whom she got the guarantee I don't know. This week I received a letter from Sigmund Rothschild of Alsfeld, in from Palestine; he writes that he got a job in the travel business. Brother-in-law Hermann recently wrote me from Africa that I should send you my greetings. Now, dear Toni, the small daughter is very cheerful and cries well, that is yet the first thing the young ones can do. I have not yet purchased a convertible sofa; I have only bought two suits and want to see how I come out with my cash. Perhaps it's OK for me to sleep without bringing a sofa; I can bring the bedding that I have here. Now, dear Herbert, you write that you have much to learn and how is it going with you in school? Irene can you speak good English? Now, little Walter, I congratulate you heartily on your tenth birthday and wish you all well. I have not yet received the authorization from Wald as of today, last week I wrote to Roth in Kaletsch, he should concern himself with me. Otherwise I don't know anything new, thus hope it goes well for you and be heartily greeted from

Your

Grandpa (Opa)

Many greetings on Malches Klara & the young ones and Hilda should not be forgotten

Stamps for a return letter are enclosed!

On the backside:

Meine Lieben!

I guess you are all in good shape, and especially what is your smallest daughter doing, what is her name and does she make good progress, also our Sophie is already three weeks in the hospital with scarlet fever. Also dear Moritz is not well, already fourteen days in the hospital I hope that he comes home this week. Also I have heard nothing from your letter as your sister-in-law does not say anything. I wrote to dear Leopold and he answered immediately. I also want to tell you promptly that we have a Jahrzeit on April 16. Lina from Rueddingshausen has received a guarantee for Bolivia but wants to first wait until Moritz arrives there. Have good holidays and hope the matzo tastes good. We have about twenty pounds of matzo. So stay healthy and many greetings and kisses.

Aunt Jenny

Letter 5, August 13, 1939

Hilda, related to Berta, is the mother of Julius and Otto Stern, my cousins. It was Otto Stern who visited Roth while in the American Army after the German surrender and forced the villagers to restore the Jewish cemetery of Roth.

To get to Shanghai was an expensive undertaking, involving all sorts of papers, approval from the Japanese (they were in control of much China at that point), and a long trip on the Trans-Siberian railroad followed by additional transport. Unfortunately no Jews from Roth made it to Shanghai.

Roth, August 13, 1939

Meine Lieben!

Got your letter and was completely surprised by your picture dear Hilda. We were delighted, as you can imagine, that you seem to have gotten much younger. The picture of dear Helen is also very good; there she makes a serious face. How long it will take until we get to Stuttgart we cannot yet know. Now there are between seven thousand and eight thousand in line, whether it goes on like this one never knows. Bluems' Hermann and Berta are going not to Brazil but to Shanghai, as one can go there without any visa. The Waldorfs are going with them and are thinking of leaving in February. I don't know what else to report. Greetings and kisses from

Your

Mother Sister-in-law and Aunt Berta

Meine Lieben!

Today Sunday morning I am writing to you first thing. We are all healthy thank God and hope the same to you. That we were pleased with the pictures you can imagine, dear Aunt you have never looked so young as in the picture. Dear Helen doesn't seem to be comfortable on the couch; she looks so serious. Louis and I were in Frankfurt this week, also your grandfather is doing well, he accompanied us. Stella Rosenberg and daughter travel every day to Frankfurt to participate in a cleaning course. Because I have nothing else to report, I send you the best greetings,

Your

Hugo

Louis sends the best greetings.

Left margin (written by Berta): The customs on the coffee came to 2.30.

At the top margin (from Berta): In the past week we received a small packet of coffee I think it came from Ida you can figure that out I want to make clear to you no one should send us anything we have enough of everything.

In the left margin (from Berta): It's good we got the pictures I take them in my hand twenty times a day to look at them. Greetings and kisses to Helen.

Letter 6, January 14, 1940

This letter is sent five months after the prior letter (August, '39). This is the first letter since the Germans attached Poland and the war had officially begun. This is the first mention by Berta asking my family to go to work on papers since much earlier.

Roth, January 14, 1940

Meine Lieben!

I take it you are all healthy, I can thank God report from us that we are in the best health. Hopefully you will have already received the letters in which I ask you for renewal of the guarantees, please take care of that as quickly as possible. What are you up to in your household dear Toni do you have enough to do? Thursday Louis was in Fronhausen. How's it going with Helen? Does she make good progress? Since I know nothing more to write, I send my hearty greetings and kisses

Your

Berta

Letter 7, March 31, 1940

Marion is Marga's daughter who is the same age as Helen. Also, this letter contains the first mention of Grandfather's illness.

Roth, March 31, 1940

Meine Lieben!

Fourteen days ago received a letter from you I wait from one day to the next. I assume you are all healthy and I can thank God also report the best health from us. In the past week we received from Klara Justus out of Amsterdam a card in which she informed that the hen and sausage she sent to us at your request, dear Hilda, did not get to us, at the same time informed us that a package with smoked meat fat and coffee was sent and this we received. Convey our best thanks for we were very happy about this, especially with the smoked meat, but henceforth you do not need don't need to send us anything. This morning we received a card from the wife of my nephew Hugo in which she informed us that she at your request dear Toni sent a package with Matzo? Is it already on its way and one with meat? I say to you best of thanks with the remark that you do not send us anything more. How is it going with dear Helen and little Marion? As you dear Hilda write Helen is very happy if someone comes from you she knows it's good with her.

After Pesach, Ilse Bluem is going to Frankfurt and a job (in an old folks' home). This week Berta Bluem wrote that your grandfather is still in bed and very weak, Louis will in the course of this week visit him here everyone is doing well. How are all the relatives? As I know nothing more to write I will close with the heartiest greetings and kisses

Your

Berta

Hearty greeting and kiss for dear Helen and all relatives

Letter 13, August 6, 1940

This is a perfect example of what I would consider a 'fluff' letter. In the context of world events at the time, it is well into the war and all Berta is talking about is how she, her friends and relatives in Germany are doing fine.

Roth, August 6, 1940

Meine Lieben! [cursive—expanded because of tearing off missing text]

Today we received an airmail letter from you dear Toni and we were happy to hear that you are all well, I was especially pleased that the Helen is such a cheerful child and can already talk so well, as you dear Toni write she and Marion [missing text]. I hope my nephew Morris is well again and that the papers are soon in order. The Bachenheimers have received no papers at all. The Blums and Goldines are doing well except for Goldine herself who is now in a hospital in Frankfurt. Joseph will go to visit her on Sunday. Ilse is a nice girl but not like Trude. Helmut und Kurt are now here on vacation as well as the child of Ida from Nauborn we are missing only you dear Walter. The Hirsche are at home on Saturday they were both here, probably they can very soon go to Stuttgart. Dear Otto when I see your picture and that which was last made here you have become there much smaller, how is that? I am surprised to hear no mention of Ida. Dear Hilda in the hot weather you probably don't go out much, right? I want to let you know we are all healthy and give you our greetings and kisses

Your

Berta

Meine Lieben!

In closing I want to add a few lines. Dear Markus you ask about your guarantee; it is totally rejected because the contribution [Verdienst] is inadequate the financial backing is insufficient for the support of too many people. Max gives a guarantee only for Louis for us however none. In Stuttgart they are very exact [genau]. Receive our best greetings.

Your

Hugo

Extra greeting to dear Helen.

Letter 17, Sept 26, 1940

This letter shows Berta's Jewish mothering of Helen and Toni, even from overseas. This is a theme that continues on as the letters progress, and I think in many ways the thought of seeing Helen was a very large motivator for my family stuck in Germany. Additionally I gather from the context that there is some concern that I am mischievous and not to be trusted.

Roth, Sept 26, 1940

Meine Lieben!

Received today the guarantees from Julius, Louis and Herman as well as your letter with picture, we were happy to see that dear Helen has quickly grown big, but I would nevertheless not leave her with dear Walter alone in the playground, I would be too anxious. It pleases me to hear that you are all healthy. Whether the papers are the way the people in Stuttgart want them we will learn when we go there. Dear Toni you write that you can still not speak much English; how is it that your children can speak English and also Markus speaks English and you are still learning - you otherwise did not have so much trouble learning something. How is it with you other ladies and gentlemen is it going better with the language, dear Hilda you will have learned it best. Please convey to my nephew our thanks for sending the guarantee I will write. I can't write before the holidays though. Last week I wrote to Max. Klara's mother now lives alone in Lohra; she has no wish to come here. More news I don't know to write.

Receive hearty greetings and kisses, from

Your

Berta

Letter 18, October 6, 1940

This letter is written over the High Holidays in 1940. It indicates that they are still thinking about and perhaps even practicing their faith. It is mentioned that they couldn't make a minyan because Herman had to leave town. I find this suspicious because Herman was the Jewish elder and very religious. I doubt he would not have left unless there was no alternative and thus I believe that he and others mentioned were forced to work by the Nazis in the surrounding towns.

Roth, October 6, 1940

Meine Lieben!

You could not really have given us greater fun than by sending us the picture of Helen and a few days later we received a picture of the dear Marion we pick up both often and would like to see more than what is in the photo. Hope you are all healthy, can from our side also report that all is well. A Minyan we did not have, Herman had to leave on the second day of the holiday for Marburg. Dear Hilda you asked what the young people do here, Joseph and Heinz go to work in Giessen, Gerdi works in a plant nursery (Gaertnerei) and Lilli does what her mother has always done. Dear Toni you can well laugh that dear Klara helps you with the stuffing stockings as that is not good work. And Helen is so cheerful and dances and sings a lot there I would like to know where she does this, pay attention to her and do not let her go out with the other children, my thoughts are always on this. Dear Toni it occurs to me I have heard you make so many worries about our guarantee, do not do this, God will help that will also come to pass. According to what I heard Julius Loewenstein will move to Frankfurt which is quite right there is really no one in Fronhausen with whom he can consult. Klara's mother was here over the holidays, she was too lonely in Lohra. For the last of the holidays Berta nee Blum and her husband are coming. I have already written to Aunt Ida. Don't know of any other news to write, I send my hearty greetings and kisses from

Your

Berta

Letter 19, December 25, 1940

This letter marks the first time that exact requirements are mentioned. This also begins a new urgency in obtaining papers. Two weeks later a near identical letter was sent by Berta re-detailing the requirements. In all we received four letters within four weeks all detailing requirements for guarantees and asking for more money as there were expirations, issues, etc. At the time, my father was making fifteen dollars per week, had to support a family of five. In addition to the Nazi red tape, there were constantly changing requirements by American immigration officials. At this point, my family was being asked by Berta to put up $2,000 per person - a near impossible task.

Roth, December 25, 1940

Meine Lieben!

After we sent the Bachenheimers guarantee to Stuttgart, they rejected all guarantees with the exception of yours dear Markus with the following explanation:

> The grounds given by your guarantors for assuming the responsibility to support [the family] are in the view of the consulate not persuasive enough for the consulate to believe that they would provide for your upkeep for a long and uncertain time period, especially, as there is no close family relationship obliging them to do so.

We are not alone, as from what we have heard they reject all guarantees that are not from very close relatives, as for example from children or siblings. If you dear Markus and Toni now put up the guarantee it would only be of use, if your income and properties in Stuttgart alone are insufficient, if you put up a deposit. Today Klara your sister from Giessen is here, and she tells us that her uncle in Stuttgart said that his daughter had to come up with US$2000 per person but that she didn't earn that much. We asked around in addition to this and we were told that you should on your side also consult with those who are familiar with the immigration requirements, for example with the Jewish Hilfsverein (aid agency). Inquire exactly, if you could perhaps put it up so it is correct, and whether an American has to co-sponsor/guarantee with you. If you cannot come up with the deposit for all of us, then put it up for one person, for Louis.

I waited a few days longer to write, I wanted to first talk to Fraulein Nathan, as I knew that her uncle was in Stuttgart. Hope that you are all healthy, we are also healthy. Dear Hilda how was your birthday and dear Helen how was yours. Dear Irene yours is coming up soon, I send you all the heartiest congratulations and hope your parents can watch you grow up with joy. Don't know anything more to write. Receive all relatives hearty greetings and kisses from your

Berta

Letter 23, February 23, 1941

Roth, February 23, 1941

Meine Lieben!

In the past week I received your letter from Toni on Jan 26 and this week from Hilda on February 18. We are happy to hear you are doing well, we are also healthy. Until today we have received no guarantee we wait every day for one, as soon as one comes we will send it to Stuttgart. Dear Hermann you write that we should write to Stuttgart, that we have already done and heretofore no answer is forthcoming; I believe only we have as much yearning for you as you for us. Before we need to go to Stuttgart, we need to have seats on a ship, if it gets to that point we will send an express post and you must inquire as to what you must do. Dear Markus your sister and her family as well as your grandpa are doing well. Dear Hilda you write that Toni has sent a small guarantee that does no good a correct one is better than a small guarantee, you must inquire, that changes too often. Otherwise everyone here is well. Sending hearty greetings and kisses

Your

Berta

Letter 24, March 4, 1941

Roth, March 4, 1941

Meine Lieben!

We were delighted to get your letter of March 1; we can report the same of us. Also your birthdays have been experienced and celebrated. As dear Helen is described to us we can imagine her very well. Got the guarantee from my niece, she is however so lowly placed that it has no value. Bachenheimers' guarantee is significantly better, as they have a good income and have nevertheless given us no answer from Stuttgart, such small guarantees have, it appears, no value; it was also that way when you were still here. Then they were also looking for big guarantees. Why is it that my niece did not put up a guarantee together with her husband, he would have had income and more capital. Such guarantees have no worth. If you can't put up a big guarantee then it's pointless. In addition you must consult with an aid agency or a shipping company because it changes so frequently, they will know if a guarantee is big enough. Don't know anything more to write. Sending hearty greetings and kisses

Your

Berta

Letter 27, April 6, 1941

Roth, April 6, 1941

Mein Lieben!

Wednesday received your letter with the document and Saturday your letter dear Hilda of February 25. That you are all healthy we are delighted to learn, I'm sorry that dear Marion was not well and I will hope she gets well soon. I would be happy if Hirsche Jetchen came to visit you so that you could speak with her. Don't be concerned about speaking English dear Hilda we will learn it together. Dear Klara you will probably be the best teacher for dear Helen. That you dear Paula and Hermann visit dear Marion every day I can very lively imagine it's good she has so well recovered. As you dear Toni write you hear so little from us I write nearly every week, it seems to us that your last letter arrived nearly five weeks ago you can imagine how we waited for it. Your niece got married with whom then? Were you not invited to the wedding dear Markus? Has Irene become tall and slender? Saturday Hirsche Herrman and his wife and their oldest daughter were here they also go soon to Stuttgart. I would like to write more but I don't know really anything of interest to you. Thus I will close. In the expectation of very soon receiving another letter from you I am with hearty greetings and kisses

Your

Berta

Letter 28, April 16, 1941

Roth, April 16, 1941

Mein Lieben!

Yesterday received a March 3 letter from you dear Hilda. We are happy to hear that you are all healthy; also with us that is also the case. The sister of the young man has been summoned to Stuttgart; they had a good guarantee there it is somewhat different. We sent all guarantees to Stuttgart and also wrote to them but still hear nothing back. If someone has a good guarantee he will be summoned if that person also has a high number. We cannot imagine why my niece sent such a bad guarantee. Louis was in Frankfurt yesterday at the Hilfsverein and [my niece] should apply to the same, also on my nephew Rudolf. We gave the Hilfsverein the name and address of Uncle Moses and the Rudolf writes to us also his address. Although to be sure we don't know if our papers were in order the ship passage came for us as we heard that all tickets were sold through February and anyone summoned to Stuttgart must already have passage booked.

The people get everything ready even when the papers are not in order; it is exactly as it was earlier with the numbers. Be careful that your money is not lost if we cannot make use of the ship passage, but it will cost something. You must make inquiries so that you know how it works with the whole immigration procedure. Get together with those people who emigrated from here, they know how the matter proceeds.

How is everything else with you? Louis learned various things in Frankfurt including that you dear Walter skipped a class in school. We were very happy about this even though we shouldn't know it. Louis visited uncle Haune and your grandpa the latter is doing well, uncle Haune not especially. More I don't know to write. Greetings and kisses to dear Helen [illegible] right hearty greetings and kisses

Your

Berta

Margin: Inquire and order the ship passage now or we will be left behind.

Letter 29, April 21, 1941

Roth, April 21, 1941

Meine Lieben!

Saturday we received word from Stuttgart that our papers are in order, and that passage by the Hapag [*Hamburg Amerikanishe Passage Aktien Gesellschaft or Hamburg American Passage Stock Company*] must be booked for us by you and you will have meanwhile received an express post, as you know one comes to Stuttgart only if has a ship passage, so make inquiries and see to it right away. Dear Hilda to our great surprise on Friday a guarantee came from your nephew in Bloomington I see that you have taken great pains, want to write to your nephew that we on Saturday got back that our papers are in order and were summoned, I will write your nephew, you dear Toni can thank my niece, as she can't understand German.

Hope you are all healthy, can report the same of us. Is dear Marion all better? Louis today is visiting your grandpa, he is doing well, your sister dear Markus was not at home. Also uncle Haune and aunt Dorchen are near at hand.

So see to it soon to book ship passage. Don't know anything further to write. Receive heartiest greetings and kisses from

Your

Berta

Letter 30, Frankfurt, May 6, 1940

Meine Lieben Alle!

Your letter of March 9 we received on the 1st of May and were very happy and joyful to learn that you are all well. The same can unfortunately not be said of me, as I have had a serious lung inflammation, thus you must excuse me for not writing for such a long time. I took ill on March 1 and was in bed for eight days; the doctor sent me to the hospital. The hospital car picked me up on March 9, and there I lay for five weeks, and received every day two or three injections. On April 15 I was again released, as I wanted to go home, but I still needed the doctor as I am too weak in the back. I cannot yet walk in the street, but food tastes good again, and thus I think I will become completely healthy and can come to you then. Dear Markus about my emigration I cannot yet say, I must first regain my health. I mean when I can again go out and go to the Hapag and ask how I should behave, I will write you if I need a new guarantee. So write me frankly whether I should send the old guarantee back, as was the case the last time with the Hapag. They said then I didn't need to send it back, it depends *on whether you don't need one if you want to create new papers.*

Dear Herbert, I am very happy that you finished school so well and also Walter I am not very conscious of my birthday. I slept through nearly every whole day in the month of March, but for your congratulations I give you my hearty thanks. Otherwise nothing is new, stay healthy and all hearty greetings

Your

Opa

Heartiest greetings on all the Malches, the Kirchhainer and Gerta

Hedwig

Letter 31, May 14, 1941

Roth, May 14, 1941

Meine Lieben!

Your letter of April 13 arrived last Thursday, and we were delighted to get it, we can also register the best health. As I have already written we received the guarantee of your nephew dear Hilda, self-evidently we have told no one, we can imagine that then several come. All of the papers that you sent for us have arrived. I take it that you paid for ship passage as soon as we get a seat on the ship, we will be summoned to Stuttgart. As you write dear Toni, dear Helen must walk you go out with her pay attention that you do not let her loose from your hand, she wants to help too, how is it that she is so afraid of strangers, does she meet with other people so rarely? Dear Klara have you so accustomed dear Helen and Marion to the pocket, that doesn't matter they want to sneak candy, that the two small ones have become good friends doesn't surprise me dear Paula we were that also always. We are very delighted that the dear young ones are diligent and frugal. You dear gentlemen young and old write to us what kinds of work you do, I have already asked but remain until now without answer. Got a letter from Aunt Ida eight days ago will write to her next week. Otherwise know nothing to write. Send hearty greetings and kisses

Your

Berta

Letter 32, May 25, 1941

Berta mentions that she is going to visit her friend Johanna in the next town over, Fronhausen. Whether she actually made the visit I do not know, but it is interesting that she had not been there in two years. Fronhausen is so close that they used to share Roth's synagogue for services.

Roth, May 25, 1941

Meine Lieben!

That you are all doing well could be inferred from your letter of April 27 which came into our possession last week to our great satisfaction we are also healthy. Can't help but wonder whether you received the express post that we sent to you through the Hapag and have ordered ship passage for us. Many thanks for your best wishes, I wish myself to celebrate my approaching birthday with you. God help my wish to be fulfilled. How much I would like to see dear little Helen and naturally all of you as well, I must be patient. Louis goes to Frankfurt to inquire at the Hapag whether they have received payment for ship passage. I must go to Fronhausen tomorrow to visit Johana; I haven't been there for two years. The Merkels' Margrit is as fat as ever, her young one is a real kid, he can say anything (can't do so well myself). Know of nothing more to put on paper, so I will close. Receive heartiest greetings and kisses.

Your Berta

Letter 33, June 8, 1941

Roth, June 8, 1941

Meine Lieben!

Your letter of May 10 is in our possession, delighted to hear you are healthy, the same can be said of us. In any case you have received the express post from the Hapag as well as my letter in which we asked you to secure ship passage for us. You must purchase passage at the Hapag because the Hilfsverien (aid agency) can no longer do so, if you have tried to book tickets through the Hilfsverein then you must cancel them. The sister of Julius Hofman wrote to Julius express mail and told him to unbook tickets. My letters in which I wrote you that the papers are in order you have at least received, and as I wrote above we must first have ship passage, make inquiries we are not the first to want to emigrate. According to what I heard Salli and Meta from Giessen went to the USA this week. As I know nothing more to write I will close, as you write us so little personal about yourselves I have nothing to answer and with us things are pretty much the same as when you were here. Live well and receive hearty greetings and kisses from your mother, grandmother, and mother-in-law and aunt,

Berta

Letter 36, July 19, 1941

Letter 34 is dated one month after the commencement Operation Barbarossa, Hitler's invasion of Russia. In many ways, this is a typical letter in which there is no mention of the war or anything else outside the normal exchange of pleasantries. Cannot send pictures out, must be physically taken out of Germany

---

Roth, July 19, 1941

Mein Lieben!

We received your letters of the 15th and 22nd of June were delighted to hear all is well with you, also I learn that you ordered passage on the ship for us and it will soon pass that with God's will we again are all together. I am delighted that you have a good position, dear Herbert, and I will hope that you dear Otto also soon have a good position… Today I made Geele (?) from our blueberries. Bluems are in the blueberries next week I will go with them. I learn from your letter dear Toni that Aunt Dina is in bed, is she better now? Tell her she should never give up. For today hearty greetings and kisses

Your

Berta

Letter 37, Frankfurt, July 28, 1941

Meine Lieben Alle!

Your dear letter of June 29 was received, and I see therefrom that you are all doing well which I can also report of myself. Dear Herbert I am delighted that you got a nice position, and to be sure you earned it. As you write you always go swimming; do not go alone, as it is better if you go swimming in the company of others. Dear Markus as you write you want to take care of all that is necessary for my emigration from there. I agree as well that this is best, as the aid agency (Hilfsverein) on this side doesn't know much about the matter. I have seen that for myself, otherwise they would not have advised the express mail. Other people say that too, that there is no great purpose to go to the aid agency. It would be good if I could go there next spring, as my money will last only one year, yet namely until July 1942 and then I don't know what will become of me. If you have received the certificate that I received from Stuttgart, that my guarantee was purchased for enough, if this should be sent to you, then write this to me, if necessary. Know nothing more new, stay healthy and be heartily greeted from your father-in-law and grandfather.

Herz

Many greetings to all the Malches the Kirchhainer and Treiser

On the backside:

Meine Lieben!

Hope you are in the best of health, which thank God can be said of us. On the emigration we don't know much here. Brother Lergold wrote me he wants to help with it and take care of everything, but I believe it's of little worth. The Hilfsverein doesn't know anything either; one must wait. So stay healthy and a thousand greetings and kisses from your dear sister, sister-in-law and aunt

Jenny

Letter 38, August 31, 1941

Ilse, the daughter of our neighbors the Bluems, had tried to make it to England and was unsuccessful. She was then sent to do forced labor in Berlin and later deported to do a death camp.

Roth, August 31, 1941

Mein Lieben!

Your letter of August 8 we received this week, were delighted to hear you are all well, I can also report the best health from all of us. Above all I send you all my love at the end of the year my heartiest congratulations, together with my most intimate wishes for your further prosperity, I will hope that we can be together next year. We were delighted by dear Helen and Marion's picture. If dear Helen breaks her toys so quickly she is not, in that respect, like you dear Toni. Otto his wife and child are doing well. Gerdi is as she was when you were here often very moody (launisch). The Bluems' Ilse is in Berlin and doing well. I am amazed that with you everything is washed, the things do not get any prettier from being washed all the time. From the letter dear Hilda that you appended for Johana she was very happy and will write back to you soon. Helen and Marion are certainly glad to be with you it seems to me you always do what they want. Hugo just tells me that you dear Markus have your birthday this week, send you a somewhat delayed but well intended hearty congratulations. Have good holidays and hearty greetings and kisses

Your Berta

Letter 40, Sept 28, 1941

I am not sure to which Stern children Berta is referring. At time of this letter there were no Sterns left in Roth. It could mean that the Nazis were bringing in Jews from other towns and placing them in Berta's house. This suspicion was aroused because it's peculiar that children have three weeks off in September/October. Additionally, it is known that the Nazis were forcing Jews to move together into single houses as the Nazis prepared the Jews for deportation to the death camps.

Roth, Sept 28, 1941

Meine Lieben!

We received your letters, delighted to hear you are well. Your letter dear Toni with the picture of dear Helen and Marion came somewhat late we were very glad to receive it also when Helen made an earnest face and yet she is very well taken, how does she actually look? In the first picture she looks like Herbert but now she no longer looks that way, I can tell you that picture gave us a lot of fun. With your lines dear young people you made us very happy. Tomorrow we get business in the house the children of the Sterns come, they have three weeks vacation, and now we are glad when they go away again. In closing I want to convey our well wishes, also everyone here is doing well. Send the hearty greetings and kisses

Your

Berta

Margin: How is it that Helen was so anxious when she met Max, is she not often in the company of other people. We received letters from all my siblings over there, greet them for me.

Letter 41, Frankfurt, October 9, 1941

Similarly to the Herman, the elder from Roth, Jenny's husband Hermann, also a very religious orthodox Jew, is forced to work on Yom Kippur.

Frankfurt, October 9, 1941

Meine Lieben Alle!

Your dear letter of September 2 received and I could tell therefrom you are fine, which makes me very glad. The same can from me also now be said. Dear Markus you write, you want to see if you can send money here from what I hear that is of course permissible, but before July 1942 you don't need to send any; I have enough to last until then, hopefully by then I can come. Dear Toni, recently I dreamed that I had arrived at your home, and that little Helen had run up to me to greet me dressed in a blue velvet dress. But the joy did not last long, I awoke and it was a dream, but that comes from the fact that the entire day I think of you and then I dream at night of you. Hopefully the hour will come when I can still see you all. Dear Herbert write to me sometime what Julius and Otto are doing, otherwise I don't know anything new, stay healthy and be all heartily greeted by your father-in-law and grandfather

Herz

Many greetings on all the Malches, all the Kirchhainer, and Treiser

On the backside:

Meine Lieben Alle!

I assume you are all doing well, which can somewhat be reported of us; our Martin was in the hospital for three weeks and came home yesterday - he had a bad foot, now, thank God, he's doing better. Now I want to give you my daily report of Rosh Hashanah. Hermann goes to work mornings at 6:30 am and comes home at 7:30, also on Yom Kippur. Our Sophie had one day free. Dear Markus Bertel was in New Jersey. He thought he could do something for our emigration, but there you need dollars. So stay healthy and let me hear from you and a thousand greetings and kisses from us all especially from your sister and sister-in-law and aunt

Jenny

Letter 42, Oct 12, 1941

Building further on letter forty, we were told that the Jews of Neustadt were sent to live with the Jews of Roth prior to their deportation. Years later, abandoned prayer books from the Jews of Neustadt were found, supporting this story.

Roth, Oct 12, 1941

Meine Lieben!

Thursday received your letters of the 20th and the 11th; we were happy to learn from them that you are well and can report the best health from us.....

The holidays went well, we have plenty of traffic from the Neustadt people I don't go to visit them often it's been a long time since they were here I was there two times but tomorrow I will go visit them again. Dear Toni make good use of the good weather and go assiduously with dear Helen on walks she can stay at home enough in the winter. Know nothing more to write. Send hearty greetings and kisses.

Your

Berta

Letter 43, Oct 27, 1941

At this time, the Germans were marching towards Moscow, and Brits and Germans bombing each other at a furious pace. Perhaps it was getting dangerous for Berta and she was afraid to write anything of substance, therefore opting to write about the weather. There's also no mention of going to Stuttgart or getting out of Germany.

Roth, Oct 27, 1941

Meine Lieben!

Even though we have heard nothing from you for fourteen days I still want to inquire as to how you are, we hope the best, we are also healthy. In the past week we got a card from Haune and Dorchen they are doing well we have not heard from your grandpa for a long time, we will write him sometime.

Dear Toni hopefully you will make use of the nice weather assiduously (fleissig) to go on walks with Helen, when there is bad weather she will have plenty of time to stay in her room. Does little Marion go with you? I have harvested everything and also spaded the yard, also washed and today I will iron. As I know nothing to write send hearty greetings and kisses.

Your

Berta

Letter 44, Nov 18, 1941

In this letter exists a change in tone; Berta is self-reflective, recognizing she asks a lot of questions. Additionally, she wants to know everything about the family in the US but volunteers almost no information about her situation or that of her friends and family in Germany.

Roth, Nov 18, 1941

Mein Lieben!

Although we this week again received no news from you I wish to inquire about how you are and hope you are all healthy from us I can report the best of health. This week we again received news from Haune and Dorchen they are healthy. I want to again inquire about Irene I have already asked frequently but have yet to receive an answer, how long has she been going to school? Does she learn to make handicrafts there or is that not done over there, one must learn something before one leaves school? I know what you think (she wants to know everything) but it is just that I am interested in everything that concerns my relatives over but especially for Irene. Does dear Helen go out often? Does she talk a lot, or is she still like you dear Toni? Dear Klara this week I wrote your niece Gretel about a young women who came from Neustadt to live here [in Roth], as she writes it is going well for them. Don't know any other news. Send you hearty greetings and kisses

Your

Berta

Send you all the heartiest greetings

Your

Hugo

Extra greeting on dear Helen

Margin (Berta): Greeting and kiss for dear Helen. Also hearty greetings for all my siblings and relatives.

Letter 45, Date Unknown

Letter forty-four is missing half of it as well as the date. The half translated makes reference to letters written to relatives and asks about health. Interestingly, the margin contains a note on the US assigned queue numbers for visa applications. The margin also notes "no need to make extra comments about Louis and Hugo." This likely refers to health issues that Berta's sons had which would have been an impediment to gaining entry into the US.

Roth, (Date unknown)

Margin:
Inquire sometime whether it might be best to send the papers to Washington. No need to make extra comments about Louis and Hugo. (Berta).

Our quota numbers are:

Mother 18981
Hugo 19089
Louis 19880

Letter 46, Date Unknown

[Note: in the before standing copy of this letter fragment (probably a 2nd page or the back of a letter) the first part of the letter is not at hand. Therefore the date of this letter fragment is not determined, but a clue is the birthday wishes for Toni's birthday (July 27).]

Roth, (Date unknown)

Julius Loewenstein advised us you could also move into an old age home (Altersheim) in Frankfurt but this is vanished. Know nothing further to write. Receive hearty greetings and kisses from your Mother sister-in-law and Aunt Berta

Meine Lieben!

I will write immediately this morning so that I will not be disturbed when visitors arrive later. Above all I send to you dear Toni on your birthday the heartiest congratulations and wish you all well. I was very happy with your lines dear Julius, but that I saw your signature again dear Irene pleased us very much. Hopefully you have meanwhile found a position dear Otto. What does your nephew Julius dear aunt that you write that he has nothing left, if the wife of Julius is not over quota she can come it will take a long time for she has a very high number still higher than Johanna and she has 38000. Dear Paula you write that it is so hard to learn English, wait till I get there and we will learn together. Anneborbs' Els [*Elsa?*] had a wedding today she married according to Church service and Heiner *[nach Kirchvers u. Heiner]* briefly and simply (in aller kuerze), he is marrying a woman from Oberhausen. On Tuesday Hermann Hammerschlag and his wife out of Treis are leaving for America. Dear Helen is quite right not to eat mash (Brei), cook her soup and meat instead, that is cheap and tastes good. Dear Markus and dear Walter as I see from your letter you were in a museum, write sometime dear Walter all that you saw there. Josef Bergenstein on vacation Junge is a Bachenheimer from Hallenberg and his grandfather stems from Rausch-Holzhausen. We have very hot weather and are looking for places to cool off. As I know nothing particular to write I will close. Receive all the heartiest greetings

Your

Hugo

Margin: Also receive from me the heartiest congratulations dear Toni and best greetings

Louis

Final Communication, Berlin, March 12, 1942

This was the last communication my family in Chicago received from Berta and her sons. It was sent by telegram via the Red Cross in Germany. Translated, it reads:

> *We are healthy, how are you? To the confirmation of Walter we send our heartiest congratulations. How is Helen? With our best greetings, Berta*

Specifically, it makes reference to my confirmation, or bar mitzvah, which was to take place in April of 1942. Toni responded on behalf of the family in Chicago on the back of the telegram, however we never heard from Berta again. With historical records, Herbert and I were able to determine that Berta, Hugo, and Louis were deported soon after this telegram arrived in Chicago.

Both sides of the original telegram are included on the following pages.

Deutsches Rotes Kreuz
Präsidium / Auslandsdienst
Berlin SW 61, Blücherplatz 2

12 MRZ 1942 * 278141

ANTRAG
an die *Agence Centrale des Prisonniers de Guerre, Genf*
— Internationales Komitee vom Roten Kreuz —
auf Nachrichtenvermittlung

REQUÊTE
de la Croix-Rouge Allemande, Présidence, Service Etranger
à l'Agence Centrale des Prisonniers de Guerre, Genève
— Comité International de la Croix-Rouge —
concernant la correspondance

1. Absender / *Expéditeur* Berta Sara Stern
Roth Kreis Marburg (Lahn)

bittet, an
prie de bien vouloir faire parvenir à Germany

2. Empfänger / *Destinataire* Herrn Markus Roth
5311 Kenwood Ave
Chicago Illinois U.S.A.

folgendes zu übermitteln / *ce qui suit:*
(Höchstzahl 25 Worte!)
(25 mots au plus!)

Wir sind gesund wie geht es bei Euch. Zur Konfirmation von Walter sende Euch die herzlichste Gratulation. Wie geht es Helen. Noch beste Grüsse

Berta

(Datum / *date*)

(Unterschrift / Signature)

3. Empfänger antwortet umseitig
Destinataire répond au verso

4. Antwort des Empfängers:
Réponse du destinataire:

(Höchstzahl 25 Worte!)
(25 mots au plus!)

Glad to have heard from you; we
are well; Helen is fine. Hppe
that you are well. Best regards
from allø of us.

Yours, Toni.

(Datum date) (Unterschrift) (Signature)

ABOUT THE AUTHOR

Walter Roth moved to Hyde Park with his father, stepmother and two siblings in the summer of 1938 after they escaped Nazi Germany. Walter attended Hyde Park High School, University of Illinois at Navy Pier and Graduated cum laude and editor of the law review from the University of Chicago Law School in 1952. He spent a year after graduation on a kibbutz in Israel. Upon his return to Chicago, he became a law clerk for Judge Luther M Swygert of the 7th circuit until 1953 when he joined the law firm of D'Ancona, Pflaum, Wyatt and Riskind. He met his wife, Chaya, soon thereafter, whom he married in Antwerp, Belgium. In addition to his professional legal practice, Walter became active in the American Jewish Congress and became president of the Midwest Region for a number of years. In that capacity, he wrote many articles about matters affecting civil rights and Zionism. He was also active in the American Jewish Historical Society, eventually becoming president. He has served as a director and a vice president of Congregation Rodfei Zedek of Hyde Park, of which he is a current member and trustee.

Walter and Chaya have 3 children - Ari, Judi and Miriam - and seven grandchildren - Isabel, Sophie, Miko, Tema, Jonah, Emma and Talia. While his children were growing up, Walter was the president of the Akiba-Schechter Jewish Day School.

Proof

Made in the USA
Charleston, SC
17 January 2013